College Workbook
The Harbrace Handbooks

Larry G. Mapp

Middle Tennessee State University

THOMSON
★
HEINLE ™

Australia   Canada   Mexico   Singapore   Spain   United Kingdom   United States

THOMSON
™
HEINLE

Hodges' Harbrace Handbook, Fifteenth Edition
The Writer's Harbrace Handbook, Second Edition
College Workbook
Larry G. Mapp

Publisher: *Michael Rosenberg*
Acquisitions Editor: *Dickson Musslewhite*
Development Editor: *Stephen Marsi*
Production Editor: *Lianne Ames*
Marketing Manager: *Katrina Byrd*
Manufacturing Manager: *Marcia Locke*
Compositor: *Nesbitt Graphics*
Project Manager: *Joan M. Flaherty*
Cover Designer: *Linda Beaupre*
Text Designer: *Brian Salisbury*
Printer: *Webcom Limited*

Printed in Canada.
1 2 3 4 5 6 7 8 9 10   06 05 04 03

For more information contact Heinle, 25 Thomson Place, Boston, MA 02210 USA, or you can visit our Internet site at http://www.heinle.com

ISBN: 0-8384-0642-4

Preface

In an attempt to group material logically and make it easier to find, we have organized the *Workbook* into five large parts. Part 1 contains units on matters of grammar, and Part 2 treats the conventions of punctuation and other mechanics of writing. Part 3 examines word selection and word use, while Part 4 addresses issues of style. Finally, Part 5 treats writing as a whole. Within these large groupings we have created units on the topics you expect. The organization of the material complements the clear explanations and helpful exercises that the *College Workbook* continues to offer, so we think you will find this an extremely useful and practical text.

The exercises now are grouped at the end of each unit for easier access. Within each exercise we have tried to create a complete unit of discourse so that the sentences fit together semantically. We believe that by writing small but whole discourses we encourage students to think in terms of complete discourses even as we instruct on issues such as punctuation or grammar.

Unit headings carry references to both *Hodges' Harbrace Handbook* and *The Writer's Harbrace Handbook.* At several junctures in the workbook we also encourage students to extend their study of a topic by consulting one of the handbooks. While the workbook has a less formal tone, its lessons are the same as the handbook's, and the two work well in tandem.

The work on this edition has been made immeasurably easier and more pleasant because of the efforts of Michell Phifer, Karen Smith, Lianne Ames, Stephen Marsi, and Joan Flaherty. I appreciate their leadership, close reading, and attention to detail.

My research assistant Melissa Blackman has provided critical editing and proofreading skills during this revision, and I appreciate her contributions to the project.

As always, I thank my wife Ann whose generosity knows no bounds.

Contents

Part 2—Punctuation and Other Mechanics of Writing

Part 3—Word Selection and Word Use

Part 4—Style

Part 5—Writing

PART 1 Grammar

UNIT 1

Parts of Sentences

Hodges': chapters 1, 12, 13, 14
Writer's: chapters 16, 17

Parts of speech

As you analyze your writing, or that of other writers, you need to learn to identify the words in sentences. Ultimately you will want to identify each word as a specific *part of speech* and as having a specific *function* in its sentence. The following chart lists the various functions words can perform in a sentence and the types of words that perform each function.

Function	Kinds of Words
Naming	Nouns and Pronouns
Predicating (stating or asserting)	Verbs
Modifying	Adjectives and Adverbs
Connecting	Prepositions and Conjunctions

The next chart summarizes the parts of speech that you will study in detail in the rest of this section (except for interjections).

Parts of Speech	Uses in Sentences	Examples
1. Verbs	Indicators of action, occurrence, or state of being	Josh *wrote* the report. Sarah *studied* the essay. They *are* students.
2. Nouns	Subjects and objects	*Josh* gave *Sarah* the *list* of *chapters.*
3. Pronouns	Substitutes for nouns	*She* will return *it* to *him* later.
4. Adjectives	Modifiers of nouns and pronouns	The *third* chapter is the *interesting* one.
5. Adverbs	Modifiers of verbs, adjectives, other adverbs, or whole clauses	presented *clearly* a *very* interesting study *entirely* too long *Indeed,* we are ready.

Parts of Speech	Uses in Sentences	Examples
6. Prepositions	Words used before nouns and pronouns to relate them to other words in the sentence	*in* a hurry *with* no thought *to* them
7. Conjunctions	Connectors of words, phrases, or clauses; may be either coordinating or subordinating	lyric poems *and* ballads before the reading *or* after it *since* the signing of the contract
8. Interjections	Expressions of emotion (unrelated grammatically to the rest of the sentence)	*Good grief!* *Ouch!* *Well,* we tried.

Verbs and predicates

Although the verb is usually the second main part of the sentence, you should master it first because the verb is the heart of the sentence. It is the one indispensable part of the sentence. Remember that a trainer can communicate with a dog using only verbs: *Sit. Stay. Fetch.*

Function The verb, as the heart of the sentence, says something about the subject; it expresses an action, an occurrence, or a state of being.

Action	Professor Wolfe *wrote* all of his life.
Occurrence	He *considered* fieldwork to be necessary.
State of Being	He *seems* to have been an inspiring teacher.

The verb also determines what kind of complement the sentence will have: either a word or words that will receive the action of the verb or a word or words that will point back to the subject in some way. If the verb is *transitive,* it transfers or passes along its action to a complement called a *direct object.*

Transitive	Matzger described field trips.
	[The transitive verb *described* passes its action along to its complement the direct object *trips.*]

If the verb is intransitive, it does not pass its action along to a complement. One kind of intransitive verb is complete in itself; it has no complement.

Intransitive	The images soared.
	[The verb *soared* is complete; it does not need a complement.]

Another type of intransitive verb is the linking verb, which links the subject with a complement that refers back to the subject. The most common linking verbs are *be* (*is, are, was, were, has been, have been, will be,* and so on), *seem,* and *appear,* as well as those that are related to the senses, such as *feel, look,* and *taste.*

| Intransitive | The images seemed original. |
| | [The linking verb *seem* calls for a complement that refers back to the subject.] |

Position The verb (underlined twice) is usually the second main part of the sentence, but in questions, emphatic sentences, and sentences that begin with *there* or *it,* the verb may come first or before the subject (underlined once).

Usual Order	Students can study off campus.
Question	Have students enrolled in off-campus courses?
Emphatic	Rare is the uncommitted student.
There	There are resemblances among the students' backgrounds.

Always look for the verb first when you are trying to match it with its subject. This practice will help you to avoid agreement errors (the use of a plural verb with a singular subject and vice versa). If you look for the subject first, you may easily choose the wrong word in a sentence like this: "The students in the research institute (is, are) studying off campus." You are much less likely to choose "institute" as the subject if you first locate the verb (is, are) *studying* and then determine who or what the verb is speaking about: the institute is not studying; the *students* are studying.

Form The verb may be recognized not only by its function and its position but also by its endings in the third person. Verbs ending in *-s* or *-es* are singular in number: he tries, she jumps, it requires. Verbs ending in *-d* or *-ed* are in the past tense: he tried, she jumped, it required. (Sometimes, however, the verb changes its form altogether in the past tense: he rides, he rode; she lies down, she lay down; it comes, it came.)

Auxiliaries (Helping Verbs) The verb may be one word or several words. The main part of the verb—the word that actually expresses the action, occurrence, or state of being—may be accompanied by auxiliaries or helping verbs—words like *has, have, should,* and *can* and forms of *be.* This cluster of verbs is referred to as a *verb phrase.* Often the parts of the verb phrase are separated.

Many students could not use the computers.

[*Not* often comes between the auxiliary and the main verb; it is a modifier, not a part of the verb, even when it appears in contractions like *don't.*]

Can you use the computers?

[In a question the parts of the verb phrase are usually separated.]

Phrasal Verbs The main verb may also be accompanied by a word like *up, down,* or *in* that functions as a part of the verb. This part of the verb is called a *particle;* the particle usually changes or adds to the meaning of the main verb.

Verb	I <u>passed</u> the stadium on my way to class.
Verb with Particle	I <u>passed</u> up a chance to go in the stadium.

The particle ordinarily follows immediately after the main verb, but it is sometimes separated from the main verb.

I <u>passed</u> the chance up.

Summary

Function	The verb expresses an action (*throw, run, talk*), an occurrence (*prevent, criticize, modify*), or a state of being (*be, seem, appear, become*).
Position	The verb is usually the second main part of the sentence ("We *photographed* the black-footed ferrets."), but it may come elsewhere, especially in questions ("*May* we *copy* the records?").
Form	In the third person (*he, she, it*), the verb shows singular number by an *-s* or *-es* ending (feed*s*, come*s*, carrie*s*) and past tense by a *-d* or *-ed* ending (solve*d*, walk*ed*, carri*ed*). Sometimes, however, the verb changes form completely in the past tense: *run, ran; buy, bought; choose, chose.* The verb may be only one word (*turned*) or several words (*has turned, will be turning, should turn in*).

Subjects, objects, and complements

All sentences except those that issue commands have a stated subject. And even in a command, the subject—*you*—is understood.

[You] Find a Web site about mammoths.

Function The subject is whom or what the sentence is about. Once you have located the verb in the sentence, you need only to ask who or what is *doing, occurring,* or *being.* Your answer will be the complete subject. To find the simple subject, ask specifically whom or what the verb is talking about.

<u>Everyone</u> in our class <u>has created</u> a Web site.

[Who has created? *Everyone in our class.* Who specifically has created? Not *in our class* but *everyone.*]

My <u>topic</u>, unlike the others, <u>was assigned</u> by the instructor.

[What has been assigned? *My topic, unlike the others.* What specifically has been assigned? Not *my* or *unlike the others* but *topic.*]

As in these examples, a word or group of words usually comes before and/or after the simple subject. Do not confuse one of these other words with the subject. If you do, you may fail to make the subject and the verb work together well; you may use a singular subject with a plural verb or vice versa. As suggested in the discussion of verbs, always identify the verb before you try to locate the subject to avoid this kind of agreement mistake.

The <u>students</u> in our class <u>are studying</u> extinct species of animals.

[The verb, *are studying,* is plural; therefore the subject must be plural too. *Students,* not *class,* is the plural subject; it is the word that answers the question "Who is studying?"]

Position   In most sentences the subject is the first main part of the sentence. But in questions, emphatic sentences, and sentences that begin with *it* or *there,* the subject follows the verb or comes in the middle of the verb phrase.

Usual Order	<u>Students</u> carefully <u>research</u> an extinct species.
Question	<u>Do</u> <u>students</u> <u>keep</u> notes on their research?
Emphatic	Very detailed <u>are</u> the students' <u>notes.</u>
There	There <u>are</u> very careful <u>notes</u> about the mammoth.

Form   Because the subject tells whom or what the sentence is about, it must be either a *noun* or *pronoun*—the two parts of speech that name people and things—or a cluster of words that functions as a noun or pronoun.

Nouns are words that name individuals or classes of people (*Claudia Barnett, tribe, jury*), places (*Nashville, parks, Venus*), things (*Pampers, candy, watch*), activities (*Little League, soccer, festival*), and concepts (*divine right of kings, endurance, conclusion*). Pronouns are words used in the place of nouns; they take their meaning from the nouns that they replace.

Nouns	The *students* brought *photographs* to class.
Pronouns	*They* brought *them* to *it.*
	[*They* replaces *students; them* replaces *photographs; it* replaces *class.*]

Some pronouns—such as *we, he,* and *who*—refer only to people; some—such as *it, something,* and *which*—refer only to things; and some—such as *each, many,* and *some*—refer to either people or things.

Like verbs, nouns have certain endings that help you identify them. But unlike verbs, nouns show the plural by an *-s* or an *-es* ending (key*s,* cave*s,* tomato*es*). Some nouns completely change their form when they are made plural (*man* ⟶ *men; leaf* ⟶ *leaves; child* ⟶ *children*). Nouns may also be recognized by the articles that frequently accompany them (*a* chair, *an* error, *the* person) and by their ability to form the possessive (child'*s* shoe, people'*s* choice, boys' dates).

Somewhat like verbs, nouns may consist of more than one word, but all the words are necessary to name the person, place, or thing being spoken of: *space shuttle, Whoopi Goldberg, Smithsonian Institution.*

Summary

Function   The subject is whom or what the sentence is about. Thus when we ask who or what specifically is responsible for the action, the occurrence, or the state of being that the verb expresses, the answer will be the simple subject.

Position   The subject is usually the first main part of the sentence (*Aldo Leopold* was an important nature writer.); however, in questions, emphatic sentences, and sentences that begin with *there* or *it,* it may come after the verb or in the middle of the verb phrase (When did *Aldo Leopold* publish *Sand County Almanac?*).

Form   Most nouns and pronouns that function as subjects undergo various changes to show plural number (*hurdle* ⟶ *hurdles; woman* ⟶ *women; I* ⟶ *we*). Noun subjects are frequently preceded by articles (*a* stone, *an* essay, *the* ledger), and both noun and pronoun subjects are often followed by words that limit their meaning (a poem *without a title;* each *of the women;* someone *in our class*). A noun subject is often made up of more than one word, especially if the noun is naming a particular person, place, or thing (*Annie Dillard, Puget Sound, Comet Hale-Bopp*).

Complements As you learn to recognize objects and other kinds of complements, remember that not every sentence has a complement.

The <u>rain</u> abruptly <u>ended</u>.

Our <u>plans</u> quickly <u>changed</u>.

Sometimes a complement is possible even if none is stated.

The <u>rain</u> abruptly <u>ended</u>.

[A complement, though it is not stated, may be added because the verb, *ended,* is a transitive verb: "The rain abruptly ended our field *trip.*"

If the sentence has a complement, it can be found by following the subject and verb with "who," "whom," or "what."

The stream <u>restoration</u> <u>is</u> a <u>success</u>.

[The restoration is what? *Success* is the complement.]

<u>It</u> <u>returns</u> the <u>stream</u> to its natural state.

[It returns what? *Stream* is the complement.]

<u>Sarah Lavery</u> <u>published</u> the <u>story</u> in 1998.

[Sarah Lavery published what? *Story* is the complement.]

Her *<u>article</u>* <u>ends</u> with an appeal for more stream restoration.

[There is no word to answer the "Who?" "Whom?" or "What?" Thus the sentence has no complement.]

Function Following a transitive verb, a complement (or complements) is a word (or words) to which the action of the verb is transferred or passed along. Three types of complements may follow transitive verbs: *direct objects, indirect objects,* and *object complements.* The direct object is the most common type of complement following a transitive verb. Sometimes it is accompanied by either an indirect object, which precedes it, or an object complement, which follows it.

Direct Object	The article includes the story of a rare fossil.
	[The action of the verb is passed along to the direct object, *story.*]
Indirect Object and Direct Object	The article gives readers a mystery.
	[The action of the verb is passed along to both the indirect object, *readers,* and the direct object, *story.* An indirect object follows a verb like *give, send, bring, buy, sell* and shows to whom or for whom the verb is doing something.]
Direct Object and Object Complement	Students call the story an inspiration.
	[The object complement, *inspiration,* is another name for the direct object, *story.* An object complement follows a verb like *name, elect, make,* and *consider.*]
Direct Object and Object Complement	Students consider the story inspirational.
	[Here the object complement, *inspirational,* is an adjective that describes the direct object, *story.*]

Note: One test for a direct object is to make the active verb passive—that is, to add a form of *be* to the main verb. The word that is the object of the active verb then becomes the subject of the passive verb.

Active	Students learned several methods for finding fossils.
Passive	Several methods for finding fossils were learned by students.
	[Note that *students,* the subject of the active verb, now follows the passive verb and is the object of the preposition *by.*]
Active	Each discovery gave students a new insight into local geography.
Passive	Students were given by each discovery a new insight into local geography.
	[*Discovery,* the subject of the active verb *gave,* now follows the passive verb and is the object of the preposition *by.*]

A complement (or complements) following a linking verb (forms of *be* and verbs like *seem, feel, appear,* and *look*) points back to the subject of the sentence; it either describes the subject or renames it in some way. Such complements are called *subject complements.* A complement that renames the subject is either a noun or pronoun; it is often referred to as a *predicate nominative* or a *predicate noun.* A complement that describes the subject is an adjective; it is often referred to as a *predicate adjective.*

Predicate Nominative	The <u>fossil</u> <u>is</u> a <u>trilobite</u>.
	[The subject complement, *trilobite,* more or less renames the subject; the fossil and the trilobite are the same object.
Predicate Adjective	<u>Lavery</u> <u>seems</u> <u>skilled</u> at interviewing.
	[The subject complement, *skilled,* describes something about the subject, *Lavery.*

Position The complement is usually the third main part of the sentence, but it may appear first in a question or in an emphatic sentence. There is no complement in a sentence that begins with the expletive *there* or *it.*

Usual order	The creek <u>bank</u> <u>seems</u> an unlikely <u>place</u> to find a fossil.
Question	Why <u>does</u> the creek <u>bank</u> <u>seem</u> an unlikely <u>place</u> to find a fossil?
Emphatic	<u>Surprising</u> indeed <u>is</u> the <u>fossil</u> on the creek bank.

Form The form of the noun complement, whether it is an object or a subject complement, is the same as the form of the subject. It can be distinguished from the subject only by its position in the sentence as the third main part of the basic formula.

Subject	Large limestone *cliffs* shade the creek.
Object	Large cedar trees cover the *cliffs.*

Pronoun subject complements have the same form as pronoun subjects: *I, he, she, we, they,* and *who.* However, many pronouns used as objects have distinct forms: *me, him, us, them,* and *whom.*

Subject Complement	The <u>writer</u> <u>is</u> <u>she</u>.
	[Compare "*She* is the writer." The subject complement has the same form that the subject would have.]
Object	<u>No</u> <u>one</u> <u>ignored</u> <u>her</u>.
	[Compare "*She* ignored everyone." The object differs in form from the subject.]

Some pronouns, like nouns, have the same form whether they are subject complements or objects—for example, *you, it, each, some, many,* and *one.*

Subject Complement	The first person to see the trilobite was *you.*
Object	The others followed *you.*

Adjectives have the same form whether they are subject complements or object complements.

Subject Complement	Jennifer was *lucky*.
Object Complement	Jennifer considered herself *lucky*.

Summary

Function   Asking the question "Who?" "Whom?" or "What?" of the subject and its verb reveals whether or not a sentence has a complement. Complements function either as objects—direct or indirect—or object complements that receive the action of transitive verbs (She wrote the *novel*.) or as subject complements that rename or describe the subjects of linking verbs (The writer was *she*.).

Position   The complement is usually the third main part of the sentence (Jennifer was *lucky*.), but in questions and emphatic sentences, the complement may be stated first (*Lucky* was Jennifer.).

Form   Nouns have the same form whether they are used as subjects, as objects, or as subject complements. Most personal pronouns have different forms as objects (*me, him, her, us, them, whom*) than they do as subject complements (*I, he, she, we, they, who*). Some pronouns have the same form whether they are used as objects or as subject complements (*you, it, each, one, some, many*). Adjectives have the same form whether they are used as subject complements (The water was *green*.) or as object complements (The students called the water *green*.).

Phrases

A phrase is a series of related words (words grouped together) that lacks a subject or a verb or both. You are already familiar with phrases that may function as the verb of a sentence—the main verb with one or more auxiliaries (*will be writing*) and the verb with a particle. Other phrases may function as a subject, an object, or a subject complement.

Verbal Phrases   The verbal phrase frequently functions as a subject or object. The main part of the verbal phrase is the verbal itself—a word that shows action, occurrence, or state of being as a verb does but that cannot function as the verb of a sentence.

Verb	The Russian surveyor <u>discovered</u> a mammoth carcass in the river.
Verbals	*discovering, to discover, having discovered*

Notice that none of the verbals in the following phrases can substitute for the verb *discovered* in a sentence.

The Russian surveyor *discovering* a mammoth carcass in the river   [a fragment]

The Russian surveyor *to discover* a mammoth carcass in the river   [a fragment]

The Russian surveyor *having discovered* a mammoth carcass in the river   [a fragment]

But such verbals, alone or with other words in verbal phrases, can function as subjects, objects, or subject complements just as individual nouns or pronouns can.

Noun	The *history of mammoths* reveals some surprising facts. [subject]
Verbal Phrase	*Studying the history of mammoths* reveals some surprising facts. [subject]
Verbal Phrase	*To study the history of mammoths* is a worthy goal. [subject]
Verbal Phrase	*Having studied the history of mammoths* makes one more appreciative of ecology in general. [subject]
Noun	I enjoy the *history of mammoths*. [object]
Verbal Phrase	I enjoy *studying the history of mammoths*. [object]
Verbal Phrase	I plan *to study the history of mammoths*. [object]
Verbal Phrase	I will never regret *having studied the history of mammoths*. [object]
Noun	His passion was *mammoths*. [subject complement]
Verbal Phrase	Her passion was *studying mammoths*. [subject complement]
Verbal Phrase	His ambition was *to study mammoths*. [subject complement]

Phrases Used as Modifiers A modifier is a word or word cluster that describes, limits, or qualifies another, thus expanding the meaning of the sentence. Adjectives are the modifiers of nouns or pronouns; adverbs are the modifiers of verbs, adjectives, other adverbs, and sometimes whole sentences. The function of an adjective or an adverb can be fulfilled by a single word or a phrase, as the following sentences demonstrate.

	1 2 3
Adjectives	*Warm* temperatures *in Siberia* melted *ancient* ice.
	[The first two adjectival modifiers (a word and a prepositional phrase, in that order) qualify the subject *temperatures*. The third adjectival modifier (a word) qualifies the complement *ice*.]

	1 2 3
Adverbs	*In 1846* the surveyor traveled *near the arctic region to gather information for the government*.
	[The first adverbial modifier (a prepositional phrase) qualifies the whole sentence. The second and third modifiers (a prepositional phrase and a verbal phrase, respectively) qualify the verb.]

Single-Word Modifiers Some authorities consider articles (*a, an,* and *the*), number words (*some, few, many,* and so on), and possessive pronouns (*my, its, your,* and so on) to be modifiers, while others call these words "noun determiners." Clearly, all three normally signal that a noun is to follow.

For *many* years, Russians had found *the* carcasses of mammoths frozen in

the ancient ice, but *a* Russian surveyor had *a* unique experience as he observed

the massive creature tumbling down *the* flooded river.

Other single-word modifiers describe some quality of or set some kind of limitation on the words they refer to.

As the *raging* waters tumbled the *giant* beast, it seemed *strangely* alive,

raising its *long, curved* tusks above the water, *desperately* reaching out with its

delicate trunk to touch the *amazed* surveyor.

[*Raging* describes *waters, giant* describes *beast, strangely* qualifies *alive, long* and *curved* describe *tusks, desperately* qualifies *reaching out, delicate* describes *trunk,* and *amazed* describes *surveyor.*]

Except when they are used as subject complements, adjective modifiers, by their very nature, are almost always found near the nouns or pronouns that they refer to. In emphatic word order, an adjective modifier may follow the noun or pronoun that it qualifies, but in usual word order the adjective precedes the word that it modifies.

| Usual Order | The *long, curved* tusks danced in the waves. |
| Emphatic | The tusks, *long* and *curved,* danced in the waves. |

Adverb modifiers usually are not so clearly tied to the words that they modify and may move around more freely in the sentence, as long as their location does not cause awkward or difficult reading.

Undeniably, the experience was shocking.

The experience, *undeniably,* was shocking

The experience was *undeniably* shocking.

The experience was shocking, *undeniably.*

Phrases as Modifiers A phrase, as you may remember, is a word cluster that lacks a subject, a verb, or both. The two types of phrase that function as modifiers are verbal phrases and prepositional phrases.

Verbal Phrases The key word in the verbal phrase is the verbal itself. Participles, which usually end in *-ing, -ed,* or *-en* and are often preceded by *having,* can function only as adjective modifiers.

The participial phrase, which consists of the participle and sometimes a modifier and an object that are part of the participle's word cluster, is frequently used to expand the basic formula of a sentence. The use of a participial phrase often avoids a series of short, choppy sentences.

Short and Choppy	The mammoth was never recovered. It probably washed into the sea.
Participial Phrase	*Never recovered,* the mammoth probably washed into the sea.

OR

The mammoth, *never recovered,* probably washed into the sea.

An infinitive phrase can function as a modifier too. Unlike a participial phrase, however, it can be used as either an adjective or adverb.

Adjectival	The desire *to recover a fully preserved mammoth* has motivated many arctic explorers.
	[The infinitive phrase modifies the subject *desire.*]
Adverbial	In 1999 an arctic explorer was able *to recover a fully preserved mammoth.*
	[The infinitive phrase modifies the predicate adjective (subject complement) *able.*]

Sometimes the verbal has its own subject. It is then called an *absolute phrase* because it does not modify a single word in the sentence but rather the entire sentence. Although an absolute phrase is not a sentence, it does have a greater degree of independence from the sentence than an ordinary verbal phrase does.

Participial Phrase	The mammoth, *discovered by reindeer herders,* was frozen in the tundra.
	[The verbal, *discovered,* modifies the subject, *mammoth,* and must stand near it in the sentence.]
Absolute Phrase	*Their first efforts having been postponed by bad weather,* herders finally removed the mammoth's tusks.
	[The verbal, *having been postponed,* has its own subject, *efforts;* thus the meaning of the phrase is clear wherever it is placed in the sentence.]

Like a participial phrase, an absolute phrase can be used effectively to combine short, choppy sentences.

Short and Choppy	The herders decided to sell the tusks. They took the tusks to the Yakoutie market.
Absolute Phrase	*Having decided to sell the tusks,* the herders took them to the Yakoutie market.

Prepositional Phrases A prepositional phrase begins with a preposition—a word like *in, of, to,* and *with*—and ends with an object, either a noun or pronoun. The preposition is the word that connects the whole phrase to one of the main parts of the sentence, to another modifier, or to the object of another prepositional phrase. (A prepositional phrase often rides piggyback on a preceding prepositional phrase.)

The first indication *of the mammoth's presence* was the massive tusks, ancient treasures made from ivory, protruding *from the tundra*. The thoughts *of recovering them, of taking them to Yakoutie,* and *of selling them,* drove the herders to work *in the dim light.* Finally they wrenched the tusks *from the skull* and loaded them *on carts.*

[The first prepositional phrase (adjectival) explains the subject, *indication;* the second (adverbial) modifies the participle, *made;* the third (adverbial) modifies the participle, *protruding.* In the second sentence, the fourth, fifth, and sixth phrases (adjectival) modify the subject, *thoughts;* the seventh (adverbial) modifies the infinitive phrase *to work.* In the third sentence, the eighth phrase modifies the verb, *wrenched;* the ninth phrase modifies the verb, *loaded.*]

Often, as in the case of *of selling them,* the prepositional phrase does not immediately follow the word it modifies. When you see a preposition (such as *of*), you know that an object ("of *selling* them") follows. In this phrase, the object of the preposition is a gerund that has its own object (*them*) and could also have a modifier (of *quickly* selling them).

There are so few prepositions that you can easily memorize a list of the most common ones. But we use again and again the prepositions that we do have, and we seldom write sentences without using at least one prepositional phrase. Notice how incomplete the meaning of the following sentences would be without the prepositional phrases that qualify the meanings of the words they modify.

The age *of the animal* can be calculated *by counting the growth rings in its ivory tusks.*

[Without the prepositional phrases the sentence reads "The age can be calculated."]

Artists carve the ivory *into artworks.*

[Without the prepositional phrases the sentence reads "Artists carve the ivory."]

Clauses (dependent, independent; restrictive, nonrestrictive)

Learning to recognize clauses will help you in analyzing sentences.

Noun Clauses A clause is a series of related words (words grouped together) that has both a subject and a verb. One kind of clause, referred to as a *main clause* or *independent clause,* can stand alone as a sentence. The other, called a *subordinate clause* or *dependent clause,* may function as a noun—either a subject or object—or as a modifier in a sentence. As nouns, subordinate clauses usually are introduced by one of these words: *who, whom, whose, which, that, whoever, whomever, what, whether, how, why,* or *where.* These introductory words are clause markers; they are printed in boldface in the following examples.

| Noun | Our discovery surprised us.   [subject] |
| Noun Clause | **What** we discovered about the villagers surprised us.   [subject] |

Noun	We reported our discovery. [object]
Noun Clause	We reported **what** we discovered about the villagers. [object]
Noun Clause	**Whoever** studies the villagers will learn **that** many of them have seen the mammoth. [subject and object]

Subordinate Clauses As the preceding examples demonstrate, one kind of subordinate clause—the noun clause—can function as a subject or object. Other kinds of subordinate clauses—the adjective clause and the adverb clause—act as modifiers.

Adjectival Clauses Adjectival clauses are introduced by a subordinator such as *who, whom, that, which,* and *whose*—often referred to as *relative pronouns*. A relative pronoun relates the rest of the words in its clause to a word in the main clause, and, as a pronoun, also serves some noun function in its own clause, often as the subject. (Remember that a clause, unlike a phrase, has both a subject and a verb.)

Bernard Buigues, *who* is a French explorer, was in the small Russian town, Yakoutie.

[The relative pronoun *who* relates the subordinate clause to the subject of the main clause, *Bernard Buigues,* and also serves as subject of the verb, *is,* in its own clause.]

An adjectival clause follows the noun or pronoun that it modifies. It cannot be moved elsewhere without confusing either the meaning or the structure of the sentence.

Correct Placement	Buigues's expeditions, *which* usually *explored Siberia,* had acquainted him with the Dolgans, a nomadic tribe.
Incorrect Placement	Buigues's expeditions had acquainted him with the Dolgans, a nomadic tribe *which* usually *explored* Siberia.

Sometimes the relative pronoun is omitted when the clause is short and no misreading could result.

With Subordinator	A frozen mammoth is a beast *that* almost every Dolgan has seen.
Without Subordinator	A frozen mammoth is a beast almost every Dolgan has seen.

Adverbial Clauses An adverbial clause is introduced by a subordinator such as *since, when, if, because, although,* and *so that.* Like the adjectival clause, the adverbial clause adds a subject and verb (and sometimes other elements) to the sentence. But unlike the relative pronoun that introduces the adjectival clause, the subordinator of an adverbial clause does not function as a main part of its own clause. The adverbial clause usually modifies the verb of the main clause, but it may also modify an adjective or adverb in the main clause.

Buigues was in the Yakoutie market *when* the Dolgan tribesmen brought in two mammoth tusks; and *because* they knew Buigues, they agreed to lead him to the frozen carcass.

[The subordinator *when* introduces the first adverbial clause which modifies the verb *was.* The subordinator *because* introduces the second adverbial clause which modifies the verb *agreed.*]

The <u>Dolgan</u> <u>are</u> as <u>nomadic</u> today *as* <u>they</u> <u>were</u> 2000 years ago.

[The subordinator *as* introduces the adverbial clause, which modifies the adjective *nomadic*.]

Unlike an adjectival clause, an adverbial clause can often move around freely in the sentence without changing the meaning or confusing the structure of the sentence.

After he found the mammoth, Buigues planned how to remove it.

Buigues, *after he found the mammoth,* planned how to remove it.

Buigues planned how to remove it *after he found the mammoth.*

Punctuation of phrases and clauses

The introductory element, which offers a variation from subject-first word order, is usually followed by a comma.

PATTERN   Introductory element, **MAIN CLAUSE**

When Buigues found the mammoth, he knew he had an important scientific discovery.

PATTERN   Adverbial clauses before independent clauses

Although her father was a struggling immigrant, he still found resources to help his family.

There is usually no comma before the adverbial clause when it follows the main clause.

He guarded the site *while he planned the excavation.*

But if the adverbial clause at the end begins with *although,* a comma is normally used.

Buigues knew the animal was intact, *although some portions of the head had been damaged.*

Some writers omit the comma after the introductory adverbial clause when the clause is very short or when it has the same subject as the main clause, but there is nothing wrong with including the comma.

If the animal were excavated it would decompose rapidly.

OR

If the animal were excavated, it would decompose rapidly.

In general, do not use a comma before an adverbial clause at the end of a sentence.

Most mammoths have been discovered *after they have become badly decomposed.*

[If the *after* clause came at the beginning of the sentence as an introductory addition, it would be followed by a comma.]

PATTERN   Introductory phrases before independent clauses

Working long hours and ignoring the harsh weather, explorers prowl the tundra in search of frozen mammoths.   [introductory verbal phrase]

In his journal and on video tapes, the explorer records his success. [introductory prepositional phrase]

The comma is often omitted after prepositional phrases if no misreading could result.

In 1999 Buigues succeeded in excavating the mammoth.

Before digging, the workers carefully planned the excavation.

A comma follows an introductory transitional expression, an interjection, and sometimes a single-word modifier.

To be thorough, they divided the site into a grid.

Yes, they also took pictures of the site with various imaging devices.

Undeterred, the crew decided to work during blizzards.

Certainly, they meant to remove the creature intact.

[Writers may or may not use a comma after an introductory word like *yet, thus,* and *certainly,* depending on how closely they feel the word is related to the rest of the sentence. If they see the word as functioning primarily for transition, they use a comma; if they see it primarily as an adverb, closely related to the verb, they do not use a comma.]

Sentence forms and function

Sentences may be analyzed by form or function. Sometimes a writer has two or more related ideas to set forth. Depending on the relationship of the ideas and on the desired emphasis, the writer may choose to express the ideas in separate sentences or to combine them in one of several ways.

Types of Sentences There are four types of sentence: *simple, compound, complex,* and *compound-complex.* The number of main and subordinate clauses in a given sentence determines its type.

Simple Sentences The simple sentence consists of only one main clause and no subordinate clauses. A simple sentence is often short but not necessarily so: one or more of the basic sentence parts—the subject, verb, or complement—may be compound and many single-word and phrase modifiers may be attached to the main clause.

Simple	Scientists examine the frozen creature for clues to its life and death.
Simple	**Searching for clues to its diet,** scientists examine the creature's hairy *coat* **looking for pollen and plant fragments.**

[The main clause, or basic formula, "scientists examine the creature's hairy coat," has been expanded by two verbal phrases (in boldface).]

Simple

A **plant** biologist *from the United States,* a specialist *in fossil pollen from France,* and a specialist *in insects from Austria* will examine the **mammoth's** coat and hide *for clues to its life.*

[The subject and the complement are compound; two single-word modifiers (in boldface) and seven prepositional phrases (in italics) expand the main clause.]

Compound Sentences A compound sentence consists of two or more main clauses (but no subordinate clauses) connected by a coordinating conjunction (*and, but, or, nor, for, so, yet*) or by a conjunctive adverb (such as *thus* and *therefore*) or other transitional expressions (such as, *as a matter of fact*). (A semicolon may substitute for the coordinating conjunction.) In a compound sentence the connecting word (in boldface below) acts like the fulcrum of a seesaw, balancing grammatically equivalent structures.

Compound

Pollen samples may provide clues to its diet, **and** insects may indicate something about the mammoth's health.

[The first main clause is balanced by the grammatically equivalent second main clause. The clauses are connected by the coordinate conjunction *and*.]

Compound

The insects may give clues about the mammoth's food; **however,** some of them may also be parasites on the mammoth.

[The conjunctive adverb, *however,* balances the first main clause against the grammatically equivalent second main clause.]

Complex Sentences A complex sentence consists of one main clause and one or more subordinate clauses. The subordinate clause in a complex sentence may function as the subject, a complement, a modifier, or the object of a preposition. As is true of the compound sentence, the complex sentence has more than one subject and verb; however, at least one of the subject-verb pairs is introduced by a subordinator such as *what, whoever, who, when,* and *if* (in boldface below), which makes its clause dependent on the main clause.

Complex

The mammoth became a time capsule **when** *it was frozen.*

[The subordinate clause functions as a modifier—as an adverb clause.]

Complex

Scientists learned from other frozen mammoths ***that they fed largely on grassland plants.***

[The subordinate clause functions as the complement (direct object).]

Complex   The <u>diet</u> of mammoths **that** *lived in North America* <u>resembled</u>
                                 the <u>diet</u> of Siberian mammoths.

                                 [The subordinate clause functions as a modifier—as an
                                 adjective clause.

Compound-Complex Sentences A compound-complex sentence consists of two or
more main clauses and at least on subordinate clause. Thus it has three or more separate
sets of subjects, verbs, and sometimes complements.

Compound-Complex   <u>Scientists</u> <u>believe</u> **that** *Siberian mammoths migrated across
                        the land bridge between Siberia and North America,* and <u>they</u>
                        <u>believe</u> **that** *both mammoth species existed on a fairly specific
                        diet* **that** *disappeared as the ice age ended.*

                        [The subordinate clauses (in italics), introduced by the
                        subordinator *that* (in boldface), function as the object of the
                        first main clause, the object of the second main clause, and a
                        modifier (adjective), respectively.]

Basic Sentence Parts

Name_____ **Score** _____

DIRECTIONS In the following sentences, the subject is underlined with one line, the verb with two lines, and the complement, when there is one, with three lines. Decide whether or not the sentence parts follow normal order (subject-verb-complement). Write 1 in the blank if they do or 2 if they do not. When you have finished, try writing in normal order three of the sentences that you have labeled 2. (To do so, you will have to change a question into a statement or omit a "there.")

EXAMPLES

Mary designed the exhibit for the museum.   _____1_____

Has Brittany heard the narration in the display?   _____2_____

1. My archaeology class toured the Smithsonian last week.   _____

2. One floor contains exciting exhibits about the Ice Age.   _____

3. Printed placards give detailed information about each exhibit.   _____

4. Many exhibits feature fossils of animals from the Ice Age.   _____

5. Which exhibit did you enjoy the most?   _____

6. Our professor pointed out the old tools and stoneware.   _____

7. Are you enjoying the tour?   _____

8. Many exhibits at the Smithsonian include sound recordings, as well.   _____

9. Several walls have displays of the plants and animals from the Ice Age.   _____

10. There is even a movie in a small theater.   _____

11. What does that movie teach?   _____

12. It teaches the story of the Ice Age.   _____

13. Many tourists frequent the museum.   _____

14. As history or archaeology buffs, the tourists travel from all over the
world.   _____

15. They enjoy exhibits about the lives of people who lived during the Ice
Age.   _____

16. How do we compare to the Ice Age people?   _____

17. It is a difficult question to answer.   _____

18. Fortunately, the Smithsonian contains a huge amount of information to
help us!   _____

19. Indeed, the <u>Smithsonian</u> <u>contains</u> <u>some</u> of the best exhibits anywhere.   _____

20. Which <u>exhibit</u> <u>should</u> <u>we</u> <u>look</u> at next?   _____

REVISIONS

1.

2.

3.

Verbs in Simple Sentences

Name_____ Score _____

DIRECTIONS In the following sentences, the subject, which is usually the first main part of the sentence, is underlined once. Underline the verb twice and enter in the blank line the word or words that make up the verb. Notice that a singular verb is used with a singular subject and a plural verb with a plural subject.

EXAMPLE

Four French boys find the Lascaux Cave.   *find*

1. The four boys are searching for a secret tunnel to Castle Lascaux.   _____

2. In 1940, during the month of September, the youths discover an opening
   at the base of a large tree.   _____

3. Casual viewers cannot see the opening because of bushes and tree roots.   _____

4. Uncertain of the depth of the natural tunnel the boys toss in stones.   _____

5. The rocks fall for several minutes.   _____

6. The four youths decide to enter the tunnel.   _____

7. They must enlarge the opening to permit their entrance.   _____

8. The four boys clear brush and trees from the tunnel.   _____

9. Squeezing through the opening, each carries a lamp.   _____

10. Darkness surrounds them in the passageway.   _____

11. To their surprise, lines and colors decorate the walls.   _____

12. Their lanterns reveal ancient paintings covering the walls.   _____

13. The stone walls contain paintings of many beasts.   _____

14. One room includes paintings of red and black bulls.   _____

15. Looming over them, the largest bull is more than five meters long.   _____

16. Many drawings depict smaller deer and wild animals.   _____

17. These smaller drawings are mixed among the paintings.   _____

18. Many images depict animals that are in motion.   _____

19. The four youths have made an incredible discovery of paintings from the
    Ice Age.   _____

20. They cannot imagine the importance of their treasure!   _____

Verbs in Simple Sentences

Name_____ **Score** _____

DIRECTIONS Fill in the blank with one of the verbs listed above the exercise. If the verb that you list has an auxiliary (helping verb) or a particle as a part of the sentence, underline that word or words. Then write the complete verb in the blank at the right.

EXAMPLE

Whitney _writes_ _about_ the Ice Age paintings in the Lascaux Cave.

writes
about

paint	refer	appear	converts	explains
fills	looks	depicts	figures	introduces
creates		inspired	incises	holds

1. She _____ photographs into slides of the paintings.   _____

2. Numbers on each of the slides _____ to extensive notes.   _____

3. For example, Whitney _____ up information on the minerals in the colors.   _____

4. One note _____ the use of charcoal and clay to make black.   _____

5. She even _____ a slide of a tool holding the pigment.   _____

6. Whitney _____ out the method for applying the pigment.   _____

7. The sharp tool _____ a line in the stone.   _____

8. The incised line _____ fresh pigment.   _____

9. The artist then _____ in the shape with a contrasting pigment.   _____

10. Some details _____ to be simple carvings in the stone.   _____

11. One of Whitney's slides _____ a tool for that purpose.   _____

12. It _____ like a modern sculpting tool.   _____

13. The slide presentation _____ us to the artists, not just to the paintings.   _____

14. What _____ the painters?   _____

15. How did they _____ on the high ceilings of the cave?   _____

Subjects in Simple Sentences Exercise 1-4

Name_____   **Score** _____

DIRECTIONS In the following sentences, the verb is underlined twice. Underline the subject once and write the word or words you have underlined on the blank line at the right. (Remember that a simple subject is sometimes made up of two or more words, which are usually capitalized, such as *Ms. Kingston, Cape Hatteras,* and *Fourth of July.*)

EXAMPLE

Marcel, Jacques, Georges, and Simon <u>discovered</u> the Lascaux cave paintings.

Marcel, Jacques, Georges, and Simon

1. <u>Do</u> you <u>live</u> near any natural caverns?   _____

2. Several more large caverns <u>have been discovered</u> near Lascaux.   _____

3. The Lascaux cavern <u>is</u> famous because of the paintings.   _____

4. The painters <u>were</u> part of the Magdalenian people.   _____

5. They <u>lived</u> in this area of France for about 8,000 years.   _____

6. Archaeologists <u>have collected</u> other relics of these people.   _____

7. They <u>made</u> very fine tools and weapons from bone.   _____

8. Many bone harpoons and spear points <u>have been found</u>.   _____

9. Professor Matzger <u>has researched</u> the Magdalenians.   _____

10. In his latest publication he <u>discusses</u> the art of the caves.   _____

11. He <u>sees</u> in their tools the same artistry as in their cave paintings.   _____

12. On his desk <u>sits</u> a small stone engraving tool.   _____

13. He <u>found</u> it inside another cave in France under a pile of rubble.   _____

14. On one end it <u>has</u> an edge for engraving outlines.   _____

15. The other end <u>is</u> round to fit in the palm of a hand.   _____

16. I <u>can imagine</u> the artist using it.   _____

17. Perhaps he <u>stood</u> on a ledge to reach a high cave wall.   _____

18. The light from a fire on the cave floor <u>cast</u> his shadow on the wall.   _____

19. He patiently and slowly <u>etched</u> the outline of a small horse into the limestone.   _____

20. Perhaps from below, a younger painter <u>watched</u> the master.   _____

Subjects and Verbs in Simple Sentences

Name_____ **Score** _____

DIRECTIONS Here are ten sentences about people related to the paintings in the Lascaux caverns, all written without people-related subjects. Rewrite each sentence with a person or people (or a personal pronoun like *he, she,* or *they*) as the subject. Underline the subject of your revised sentence with one line and the verb with two lines. When you have finished revising the sentences, decide which version you think is easier and more interesting to read.

EXAMPLE

The caverns at Lascaux were discovered by four adventurous French youths.

Four adventurous French <u>youths</u> <u><u>discovered</u></u> the caverns at Lascaux.

1. The caves record animals important in the lives of Ice Age people.

2. The first room of the caverns is known to experts as the Bull Room.

3. Several drawings of aurochs, a massive ancestor of modern oxen, were made by the ancient artists.

4. Tools of stone and bone were used.

5. The caves have become for scientists windows into the Ice Age.

6. A recent expedition to the caves was lead by Professor Matzger.

7. No new finds were made by the team of four students and their teacher.

8. However, a dramatic photographic record of the cave paintings was brought back.

9. Much of our class discussion has centered on the identities of the animals in the paintings.

10. Some of the horses in the paintings have been compared to a rare horse now found in Asia.

Subjects, Verbs, and Complements
in Simple Sentences

Exercise 1-6

Name_____   Score _____

DIRECTIONS In the following sentences, underline the simple subject once, the verb twice, and the simple complement or complements three times. Write *subject* on the blank line if the complement (or complements) refers back to the subject; write *object* if the complement (or complements) receives the action of the verb. If there is no complement, leave the blank line empty.

EXAMPLE

In recent years scientists have created a system to protect the caves
at Lascaux.   *object*

1. The outbreak of the second world war protected the Lascaux cave in the
   mid-1940s.   _____

2. After the war people began visiting in great numbers.   _____

3. Visitors to the cave almost destroyed it.   _____

4. The ecosystem of caves was poorly understood at that time.   _____

5. About six hundred people visited the cave each day beginning in July
   of 1948.   _____

6. Each of the visitors exhaled carbon dioxide.   _____

7. And each visitor contributed heat to the underground environment.   _____

8. In combination these pollutants threatened the existence of the paintings. _____

9. Air warmed by visitors formed water droplets on cave walls.   _____

10. The water droplets slowly eroded the paintings.   _____

11. A mechanical system was installed to control the air in the cave.   _____

12. The system regularly renewed the air in the cave.   _____

13. Ironically, the system also encouraged more visitors.   _____

14. As many as 1,500 visitors entered the cave each day in the 1960s.   _____

15. Guides soon noticed green spots appearing on the walls.   _____

16. Analysis revealed colonies of bacteria and algae on the paintings.   _____

17. France's minister of cultural affairs acted quickly.   _____

18. He closed the caves to the public.   _____

19. A committee of scientists convened to discuss the problem.   _____

20. They soon concocted a plan to protect the cave.   _____

Verbal Phrases as Subjects, Direct Objects, and Subject Complements

Exercise 1-7

Name_____   Score _____

DIRECTIONS Each of the following sentences contains one or more verbal phrases functioning as subject, direct object, or subject complement. First, underline such verbal phrases. Then write on the blank line (1) *S* for a phrase functioning as the subject of the sentence, (2) *DO* for a phrase functioning as a direct object, (3) *SC* for a phrase functioning as a subject complement. If you write two or more things in the blank, use dashes between them. (Be sure to look for the main verb of the sentence before you try to identify the subject, direct object, and subject complement.)

EXAMPLE

We want <u>to observe the public's effect on the paintings</u>.   *DO*

1. To study the paintings' deterioration is helpful.   _____

2. Allowing the public in the caves began to introduce various pollutants and to increase the temperature.   _____

3. These problems started to destroy the paintings.   _____

4. Officials encouraged cleaning of visitors' shoes.   _____

5. To keep them clean lowered the rate of pollution.   _____

6. To allow destruction was a tragedy.   _____

7. Keeping the paintings safe was crucial.   _____

8. Archaeologists and the public agreed to save them.   _____

9. Killing the algae and bacteria required using antibiotics and formaldehyde.   _____

10. Using special lighting helps, as well.   _____

11. To allow only scientists and special visitors requires careful planning.   _____

12. Fortunately, implementing these steps helps to save the paintings.   _____

13. To determine the value of the paintings is to attempt the impossible.   _____

14. Monitoring their condition carefully may preserve them another 17,000 years.   _____

15. Studying the remarkable paintings is to establish kinship with our prehistoric ancestors.   _____

Word and Phrase Modifiers:
Adjectives and Adverbs

Exercise 1-8

Name_____ Score _____

DIRECTIONS In each of the following sentences, the word in italics is qualified by one or more single-word and/or phrase modifiers. First underline these modifiers; then draw an arrow from each one to the italicized word. Do not underline or draw an arrow from the articles—*a, an,* and *the.* Write *adj* in the blank if the modifier or modifiers are functioning as adjectives and *adv* if the modifier or modifiers are functioning as adverbs. Notice how the modifiers make the italicized words more exact in meaning.

EXAMPLES

The most commonly represented *animal* in the paintings is the horse.   *adj*

Several hundred paintings of horses brightly *decorate* the walls.   *adv*

1. This clearly demonstrates the *importance* of the horse to Magdalenian culture.   _____

2. The *shapes* of these horses look familiar.   _____

3. *Think* about a horse drawn by a great modern artist such as Picasso.   _____

4. Picasso actually *saw* the paintings and found them inspiring.   _____

5. Scientists also suggest a *similarity* between the paintings and an endangered wild horse.   _____

6. The contemporary counterpart last *flourished* on the steppes of Mongolia.   _____

7. The Przewalski is the last surviving wild *ancestor* of the domestic horse.   _____

8. All other horses *descend* from previously domesticated horses.   _____

9. The Przewalski has a small, robust *build* and an upright mane.   _____

10. It is a horse with coloration *ranging* from sandy, to dun, to reddish bay.   _____

11. It is a difficult *horse* to tame.   _____

12. The Przewalski Foundation *has managed* to preserve the Przewalski.   _____

13. The Foundation *has* a very educational Web site at http://www.treemail.nl/takh/.   _____

14. The *drawing* of a Przewalski on the Web site resembles drawings at Lascaux.   _____

15. The distinctive upright mane *catches* one's eye immediately.   _____

Subordinate Clause Modifiers:
Adjectives and Adverbs

Exercise 1-9

Name_____   Score _____

DIRECTIONS Write *adj* in the blank if the italicized clause is an adjective modifier and *adv* if it is an adverb modifier. (To test your classification, try moving the italicized clause to different places in its sentence; notice whether the new arrangement affects the meaning or the structure of the sentence. If the movement of the clause affects either the meaning or the structure of the sentence, you know that it is an adjective clause.)

EXAMPLE

When the Lascaux caves were being painted, horses freely roamed the landscape.   *adv*

1. The horses resembled the rare Przewalski *that in recent years has been saved from extinction.*   _____

2. The Lascaux painters depicted the horse *because they hunted it.*   _____

3. They also drew it with a skill *that demonstrates their respect for its beauty.*   _____

4. Wild horses must have bedeviled early farmers *who needed to keep horses from their crops.*   _____

5. *As the farmers appropriated more land,* they eliminated grazing area for horses.   _____

6. The end of the Ice Age brought more pressure on the horse *when forests began to replace the open grasslands of the steppes.*   _____

7. *Although they were being hunted heavily,* in the fourteenth and fifteenth centuries herds of horses still roamed many parts of Europe.   _____

8. By the nineteenth century the herds *that existed in Poland and Southern Russia* represented the last wild populations.   _____

9. *When the Czar sent Colonel Nicola Przewalski to central Asia,* he set in motion the eventual rescue of the remaining wild horses.   _____

10. Colonel Przewalski eventually found small herds of horses *that lived on the edge of the Gobi Desert.*   _____

11. Earlier western explorers *whose discoveries had not been publicized* actually had found these horses.   _____

12. Word of the colonel's discovery quickly spread across Europe and America among people *who were interested in owning specimens of the horse.*   _____

13. A Russian named Asonov *who was a dealer in exotic animals* organized the first expedition to capture the horses.   _____

14. *Because the adults were shy and fast,* Asonov failed.   _____

15. He decided to concentrate on foals *that could not escape his trappers.*   _____

16. *Although he eventually captured two foals,* they died shortly after capture.   _____

17. Another trapper succeeded in keeping alive some foals *because he quickly placed them with domestic mares.*   _____

18. The domestic mares *who had recently borne foals* accepted the wild foals as their own.   _____

19. In 1900 the trappers gave four foals to Czar Nicholas II *who hoped to breed them.*   _____

20. *Because the returned animals were carefully bred,* they stand a good chance of producing a viable wild population.   _____

Compound Subjects and Verbs
and Compound Sentences

Exercise 1-10

Name_____ Score _____

DIRECTIONS Underline the simple subject or subjects in each of the following main clauses once and the verb or verbs twice. If the sentence is a compound sentence, insert an inverted caret (∨) between the two main clauses. (Notice that the main clauses are correctly joined by a comma plus a coordinating conjunction, by a semicolon, or by a semicolon plus a conjunctive adverb or transitional phrase.) In the blank write *sub* if the subject is compound, *verb* if the verb is compound, and *CS* if the sentence is compound.

EXAMPLE

Horse lovers wanted to discover the fate of the Caspian horse
and hoped to find a living specimen.   *verb*

Carvings of the Caspian horse were common in the Persian Empire
beginning in the fifth century B.C., ∨ but reference to them stopped
about 1200 years ago   *CS*

1. The Caspian horse is native to Iran but was thought to be extinct.   _____

2. Rumors of small horses in the Elburz mountains in northern Iran reached
   an American living in Iran in 1965, so she decided to investigate.   _____

3. She found a herd of about thirty animals running wild; they looked
   like small versions of Arabian horses.   _____

4. She captured thirteen animals and brought them back for testing.   _____

5. Medical and zoological experts examined the horses and agreed
   on their identity.   _____

6. They were the forebears of Arab horses; they were the ancestors of all
   the Arab breeds.   _____

7. Ernest attempts to salvage the breed ensued; however, the unpredictable
   political nature of the area greatly affected these efforts.   _____

8. With the help of Prince Philip of England, several Caspians were
   exported to Europe in the 1970s and were established as a small
   breeding population.   _____

9. Much of the population in Iran died during the Iran-Iraq war, but
   stubborn efforts saved a few.   _____

10. Some of those animals were smuggled out of the country; however,
    only a few hundred now exist worldwide.   _____

Subjects and Verbs in Main and Subordinate Clauses: Complex Sentences

Exercise 1-11

Name_____ Score _____

DIRECTIONS Each sentence below contains one main clause and one subordinate clause—each clause, of course, with its own subject and verb. Underline the subjects once and the verbs twice. In the blank, write the subordinator that introduces the subordinate clause. (Remember that a relative pronoun subordinator—for instance, *who, whom, that, which*—often serves as the subject or complement of its own clause. Remember also that an entire subordinate clause may serve as the subject or complement of a main clause.)

EXAMPLES

Jennifer wrote her paper on wild horses because she had seen a herd of them in Oregon.

because

She had seen the Kiger mustang herd that roams an area of southeast Oregon.

that

1. Because she also knew of the connection between the Kiger mustangs and the earliest horses brought to the Americas from Spain, Jennifer started her research on this topic.

_____

2. She discovered that Dr. Ray d'Andrade had done research in Portugal.

_____

3. The "marismeno" is the wild Iberian horse that had found its last refuge in swamps and along river bottoms.

_____

4. In 1920, Dr. d'Andrade believed that he could ensure their surivival after finding a pure strain of them along the river Sorraia in southern Portugal.

_____

5. After he brought the small band of Sorraia horses to his farm, Dr. d'Andrade made them breeding stock to preserve the species.

_____

6. Because only a few hundred horses remain from Dr. d'Andrade's herd, horse experts were thrilled that some American mustangs might carry the herd's genes.

_____

7. They believed that the DNA might help to preserve the population of horses.

_____

8. That some American mustangs are perfect or nearly perfect examples of the Sorraia horse is exciting.

_____

9. If they are, then they might provide genetic material to save the beautiful creatures from extinction.

_____

10. Jennifer decided that her paper would focus on Dr. d'Andrade and his preservation of this marvelous species.

_____

Subordinate (Dependent) Clauses:
Functions in Sentences

Name_____ **Score** _____

DIRECTIONS Classify each italicized subordinate clause in the following sentences as a subject (*S*), a complement (*C*), or a modifier (*M*). As you do the exercise, notice the subordinator that introduces the clause.

EXAMPLE

Jennifer learned *that some wild Spanish mustangs still roam America.*   *C*

1. The Wild Free-Roaming Horse and Burro Act *that Congress passed in 1971* protects these living symbols of the old west.   _____

2. The Bureau of Land Management (BLM) manages several areas *that contain wild horses.*   _____

3. Jennifer visited the Kiger Habitat Management Area (KHMA), *which includes 37,000 acres in southern Oregon.*   _____

4. The herd of wild horses *that lives on the KHMA* fluctuates between 50 and 80 animals.   _____

5. *That these Kiger mustangs bear a striking resemblance to the Sorraia horse in Iberia* is quickly apparent.   _____

6. They have the coloration and markings *that define the Sorraia.*   _____

7. *Because they share the striking dun coloration of the Sorraia,* they are beautiful horses.   _____

8. Jennifer has a photograph *that shows the horses standing peacefully against a backdrop of evergreens.*   _____

9. Jennifer knows *that the herd increases by about twenty per cent each year and must be managed carefully.*   _____

10. *If the numbers are not controlled,* the horses will begin to destroy their habitat.   _____

11. Periodically some horses are separated from the herd and taken to the Burns Wild Horse Corrals *where the public can adopt them.*   _____

12. *Since the Kiger mustangs are known as intelligent and adaptable horses,* they are in high demand.   _____

13. The BLM also swaps horses among herds, a process *that promotes a healthier gene pool.*   _____

14. Jennifer's photographs also illustrate the markings *that are common to Kiger mustangs*.   _____

15. Some of them show zebra stripes on their legs, a marking *that is common on other wild horses*.   _____

16. She had seen those markings on a wild Asian horse *that she had studied in a London zoo*.   _____

17. Kigers also have a dorsal stripe *that reminds her of the stripes on Przewalski horses*.   _____

18. However, the Kiger mustangs are delicate in appearance, a trait *that they have inherited from their Iberian ancestors*.   _____

19. With finely shaped muzzles and hooked ears, they have the conformation *that characterizes the Sorraia*.   _____

20. *When we are in Oregon this summer*, we will visit the Kiber mustangs.   _____

UNIT 2

Sentence Boundary Problems

Hodges': chapters 2, 3, 13, 35
Writer's: chapters 18, 19

Sentence fragments

Once you become aware of the parts of the sentence, you will sense the difference between a complete sentence and an incomplete one, a fragment. Although fragments are usually not a clear way to communicate with your reader, they may be effective, and even necessary, in a few instances, particularly in answering questions, stating exclamations, and recording dialogue.

Question and Fragment Answer	Did the students in your class enjoy reading Brian Griffin's *Sparkman and Other Stories? Yes, especially* because he spoke to our class about writing it.
Sentence and Fragment	My teacher knew that Griffin was speaking on campus, and he asked him to set aside an hour for my class. *How lucky for you!* [an exclamation]
Dialogue	*"Sparkman and Other Stories* includes stories about Griffin's childhood,"* my teacher said. *"And about the end of that childhood."*

Fragments are used in dialogue simply to record people's speech patterns. The fragment used in answering a question or in stating an exclamation allows an idea to be communicated without repeating most of the preceding sentence.

Effective sentence fragments, like those used in answering questions, stating exclamations, and recording dialogue, are written intentionally. The very shortness of most fragments calls attention to them; thus they are used for emphasis. Ineffective fragments, however, are rarely written intentionally. Rather they are written because the writer could not sense the difference between a sentence part and a complete sentence.

Learn to sense the difference between a phrase, especially a verbal phrase, and a sentence. Any sentence becomes a fragment when the verb is replaced by a verbal.

Sentence	The importance of the written word *was* the theme of his talk.

| Verbal Phrases | The importance of the written word *being* the theme of his talk. The importance of the written word *having been* the theme of his talk. |

Sometimes a prepositional phrase is incorrectly punctuated as a sentence, usually because the phrase either is very long or is introduced by words like *for example* and *such as*.

| Sentence | We were impressed by Griffin's successes in other kinds of writing. |
| Prepositional Phrases | For example, as a poet. And as an editor. |

An appositive is a word or word group following a noun or pronoun that defines or restates the noun or pronoun. An appositive cannot stand alone as a sentence.

| Sentence | Griffin's appearance on campus coincided with the grand opening of the new library. |
| Appositive | A grand new building holding two million volumes. |

Another common fragment is caused by the separation of the two parts of a compound predicate.

| Sentence | Sharon Olds was on campus the week after Griffin. |
| Predicate | And spoke to my creative writing class about her collection of poems, *The Dead and the Living*. |

Learn to sense the difference between a subordinate clause and a sentence.

Any sentence can be made a fragment by inserting a subordinator before or after the subject.

Sentence	During The Southern Festival of Books Ernest Gaines spoke to my creative writing class.
Subordinate Clause	During The Southern Festival of Books *after* Ernest Gaines spoke to my creative writing class.
	During The Southern Festival of Books Ernest Gaines *who* spoke to my creative writing class.

Learn the best way to correct a fragment.

An obvious way to correct a fragment is to supply the missing part—to make the fragment into a sentence. But most fragments are best corrected by reconnecting them to the sentences they belong with. Examine the following paragraph in which the word groups that are likely to be written incorrectly as fragments are printed in italics.

Both Sharon Olds and Ernest Gaines read from their work *and answered questions from the audience. If any theme was woven through both speakers' comments,* it was the critical importance of education, *of being able to read, to write, and to think well. During Olds's session,* she also read several of her poems, and I felt as if I were hearing them for the first time.

Comma splices and fused sentences (run-ons)

Learn the standard ways to link two closely related main clauses.

In Unit 1 you studied the two main ways to expand a sentence—subordination and coordination. Subordination often requires the use of a comma or commas. Coordination, too, requires a comma when two main clauses are connected by a coordinating conjunction—*and, but, or, nor, for, so,* and *yet.*

The first draft of the review was due yesterday, *but* we asked for an extension.

If the coordinating conjunction is removed, the two main clauses may still be connected; however, the standard mark of punctuation between the two clauses then becomes the semicolon.

The first draft of the review was due yesterday; we asked for an extension.

Even if another type of connective—a conjunctive adverb like *then, therefore,* and *however*—is inserted between the main clauses, a semicolon is still the standard mark of punctuation to be used after the first main clause.

The first draft of the review was due yesterday; *however,* we asked for an extension.

If a comma is used between two main clauses not connected by a coordinating conjunction, the sentence contains a *comma splice.* In other words, the comma has been made to perform a function that standard usage has not given it.

Comma Splice	The first draft of the review was due yesterday, we asked for an extension.
Comma Splice	The first draft of the review was due yesterday, *however,* we asked for an extension.

Some students feel they can avoid comma splices by omitting all commas from their writing. And they are right. But in so doing they violate standard practices of punctuation even further. Instead of writing comma-splice sentences, they write *fused* (or run-together) sentences. And fused sentences are even more ineffective than comma-splice sentences because they are more difficult to understand at first reading.

Fused Sentence	A novel by Alice Munro won the National Book Award she accepted the award at the ceremony in New York.

The standard punctuation of two main clauses not connected by a coordinating conjunction is the semicolon.

A novel by Alice Munro won the National Book Award; she accepted the award at the ceremony in New York.

[The semicolon acts like the fulcrum of a seesaw with the idea in one main clause balanced by the idea in the other.]

There are two other ways to avoid a comma-splice or fused sentence.

Two Sentences	A novel by Alice Munro won the National Book Award. She accepted the award at the ceremony in New York.
	[Placing the two ideas in separate sentences emphasizes them equally.]
Subordination	After a novel by Alice Munro won the National Book Award, she accepted the award at the ceremony in New York.
	[Subordinating one of the ideas establishes a cause-and-effect relationship.]

The standard punctuation of two main clauses connected by a conjunctive adverb or a transitional phrase is the semicolon.

Writers seldom win the Booker Prize twice; *however,* J. M. Coetzee won it in 1983 and again in 1999.

Coetzee produces books very slowly; *in fact,* he took five years to produce his latest novel, *Disgrace.*

Notice that a conjunctive adverb or a transitional phrase may also be placed in the middle of a main clause and that the standard marks of punctuation are then commas.

Coetzee's ability to examine the complexities of post-apartheid South Africa, *however,* is unparalleled.

He is, *in fact,* the most powerful voice among South African writers.

The standard mark of punctuation for a divided quotation made up of two main clauses is the semicolon or an end mark (a period, question mark, or exclamation point).

"*Disgrace* explores the furthest reaches of what it means to be human," says the reviewer for the *Sunday Telegraph*; "it is at the frontier of world literature."

"*Disgrace* explores the furthest reaches of what it means to be human," says the reviewer for the *Sunday Telegraph*. "It is at the frontier of world literature."

Sentence Boundary Problems   Exercise 2-1

Name_____ Score _____

DIRECTIONS In the following word groups, underline each subject with one straight line, each verb with two straight lines, and each verbal with a wavy line. If a word group contains no true subject and/or verb for a main clause, indicate an incomplete sentence by writing *frag* in the blank for subject, verb, or both. Notice that a sentence may have both a verb and one or more verbals.

EXAMPLE

	SUBJECT	VERB
After studying David Lavery's essay on the life of Owen Barfield.	Frag	Frag

1. My roommate constantly reading mystery novels. _____

2. Her bedside lamp left on late into the night. _____

3. I envision the plots still dancing in her head. _____

4. Her following clues instead of counting sheep. _____

5. Having been born in Berkeley she loves stories with a California setting. _____

6. Having access to many good book stores. _____

7. She started reading mysteries in high school. _____

8. I flew home with her last month, wanting to see some of California. _____

9. Cody's Books featuring a different writer almost every week. _____

10. Bharati Mukherjee reading from her latest novel that week. _____

11. A story exploring the condition of an immigrant from India. _____

12. Having visited Black Oak Books, my roommate carried a bag filled with paperback books. _____

13. Her earnest attempt at saving and stretching her allowance. _____

14. Remembering a sign—"Buy one and get one free." _____

15. Other signs advertising bargains on used books. _____

16. She, being sure of not returning to Black Oak for months. _____

17. Seeing the happy look on her face, I knew she had made a wise choice. _____

18. Of her being a reader, of me not being a reader. _____

19. I envied my roommate's reading habits. _____

20. A reader finding pleasure more easily than I could. _____

Sentence Boundary Problems

Name_____ Score _____

DIRECTIONS In the following word groups underline each subject with one straight line, each verb with two straight lines, and each subordinator with a wavy line. (Remember that a subordinator like *who, which,* or *that* may also be the subject of its own clause.) If the word group has only a subordinate clause or clauses, write *frag* in the blank to indicate an incomplete sentence. If the word group has no subordinate clause or has a subordinate clause plus a main, or independent clause, write *C* in the blank to indicate a complete sentence.

EXAMPLES

When Ernest Gaines wrote *A Lesson Before Dying*.   *frag*

He modeled the setting after the Louisiana parish where he was born.   *C*

1. When he spoke to my literature class.   _____

2. He told us about New Roads and Pointe Coupée Parish in
   Louisiana where he was born.   _____

3. Those memories became Bayonne and St. Raphael
   Parish which are the setting of *A Lesson Before Dying*.   _____

4. When we read about Henri Pichot's sugar cane fields.   _____

5. We were reading about cane fields in which Gaines worked as a child.   _____

6. When he was older he moved to California and began studying
   in the local library.   _____

7. Because he was trying to stay off the streets and out of trouble.   _____

8. He knew that by reading and studying, he could learn more
   about his past.   _____

9. Gaines says that he "was trying to . . . find [himself] through
   literature" as he worked alone in the library.   _____

10. Because the reading connected him to the places and people he
    had left in Louisiana.   _____

11. He soon wrote his own novel that was rejected by publishers.   _____

12. He was only sixteen when he wrote the first novel.   _____

13. Gaines, although the novel was not published.   _____

14. He learned from the experience what reading could inspire in him.   _____

15. Although he was devoted to reading.   _____

Sentence Boundary Problems

Name_____   **Score** _____

DIRECTIONS In the following paragraphs are ten fragments of various types. First, circle the numbers that stand in front of fragments, then revise the fragments by attaching them to the sentences to which they belong.

¹We discussed in our last class the comment from Ernest Gaines. ²That in *A Lesson Before Dying* he explores the question. ³"What would I do if I knew exactly how and when I would die?" ⁴In the novel Jefferson is wrongly accused and found guilty of murdering a man. ⁵When he is placed on death row. ⁶Jefferson has to confront the awful question every day until his execution.

⁷Grant Wiggins is the teacher in Jefferson's poor community. ⁸Who reluctantly accepts the task of helping Jefferson learn to die like a man. ⁹Much of the story concerns the interplay of these two men. ¹⁰One college educated and articulate. ¹¹The other nearly illiterate and unaccustomed to self-examination. ¹²As is so often the case in a Gaines story. ¹³The relationship between the characters develops in surprising ways. ¹⁴As Grant soon knows. ¹⁵He cannot teach Jefferson how to die. ¹⁶Because he, Grant, does not know how to live. ¹⁷So their two stories develop in parallel fashion. ¹⁸In order to help Jefferson. ¹⁹Grant has to learn the ways he has failed himself, his family, and his community.

Fragments: Effective and Ineffective

Exercise 2-4

Name_____ Score _____

DIRECTIONS The following paragraphs include five effective fragments and nineteen ineffective fragments, incomplete sentences that the writer did not plan. Circle the number that stands in front of each fragment. Then revise the ineffective fragments either by rewriting them as complete sentences or by connecting them to the sentences they belong with. Place an X by the number of each effective fragment. After completing the exercise, discuss with your class how to identify an effective fragment.

¹When Ernest Gaines teaches classes of aspiring writers. ²He gives them simple advice. ³Read. ⁴And write. ⁵He also advises them to look at their world. ⁶Very closely. ⁷At the world under their feet as they stroll across the quadrangle. ⁸Beside their cars as they whirl down the highway. ⁹Overhead as they walk to class.

¹⁰Crys and I decided to try Mr. Gaines's advice and look more carefully at our worlds and then try to name them with the carefully chosen concrete and powerful imagery he employs. ¹¹On our way to Jones Hall today. ¹²She stopped and knelt in a patch of clover under the big cedar that shades the walk. ¹³Holding her books against her chest with her left hand. ¹⁴She reached forward and with her right hand quickly plucked three stems. ¹⁵Each a four-leaf clover. ¹⁶She had been watching so closely that she had noticed them from several feet away. ¹⁷I have seen her do this many times. ¹⁸Yet I have never found a four leaf-clover without her help. ¹⁹I am unable to see the four-leaf clusters. ²⁰Unless I kneel and almost take each one in hand to examine it. ²¹Somehow she can find the four-leaf pattern against the jumble of all those apparently identical green leaves.

²²We then sat on the steps of the library and watched students. ²³Occasionally making notes about details we wanted to remember. ²⁴Or about conversations we overheard. ²⁵I spent several minutes trying to decide how to describe three boys. ²⁶Who were using the

loading dock as a skateboard ramp. [27]Two of them did everything very casually. [28]Even when they fell. [29]They picked themselves up very slowly. [30]Never checking themselves for bruises or scrapes. [31]And picked up their boards with one hand. [32]Spinning them quickly as they set them down for another ride. [33]Never smiling. [34]The other boy was more joyful. [35]More aware of the crowd watching him. [36]Laughing when he made a good move or when he fell. [37]Sitting on the ground for several minutes after one fall, rubbing his knees. [38]Obviously in pain from hitting the side of the ramp. [39]I wondered if the other two thought he was not cool because he was so openly emotional. [40]Or if they envied his ability to have fun.

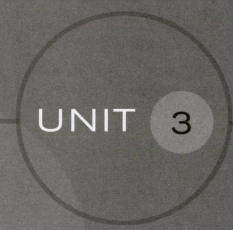

UNIT 3

Verbs

Hodges': chapter 7
Writer's: chapters 16, 22

Principal parts of verbs

You will remember from Unit 1 that the verb is the most essential part of the basic formula for a sentence. Sentences may be written without subjects—though few are, of course. And sentences are frequently written without complements. But without a verb, there is no sentence.

To use verbs correctly, you must know how to make the present tense of the verbs agree with their subjects in number and how to choose the right tense of the verbs to express the time that you intend: present, past, future, present perfect, past perfect, or future perfect.

Verbs have three main tenses—present, past, and future—and three secondary tenses—present perfect, past perfect, and future perfect. A verb's ending (called its *inflection*) and/or the helping verb or verbs used with it determine the verb's tense.

Present	write
Past	wrote
Future	will write
Present Perfect	has or have written
Past Perfect	had written
Future Perfect	will have written

Actually there are several ways to form a given tense in English. For the past tense, for example, you could write any of these forms:

She *wrote* one-act plays.

She *was writing* one-act plays.   [continuing past time]

She *did write* one-act plays.

[Emphatic. Notice that this form of the past tenses uses *did* plus the present form of the main verb, *write.*]

She *used to write* one-act plays.

[*Used to* (NOT the common misspelling, *use to*) suggests an action that no longer occurs.]

Most verbs are *regular* verbs; that is, they form their tenses in a predictable way. The *-ed* ending is used for the past tense and all the perfect tenses, including the past participle form of a verbal. The *-ing* ending is used to form the progressive and the present participle.

Past	She *entered* the piano competition.
Present Perfect	She *has entered* the piano competition.
Past Perfect	She *had entered* the piano competition before she strained a muscle in her hand.
Future Perfect	After only two years of training she *will have entered* three major piano competitions.
Past Participle	*Having entered* the competition, she nervously watched the other competitors.
Progressive	She *is entering* the competition. [also *was entering, has been entering, had been entering, will have been entering*]
Present Participle	*Entering* the competition, she begins the next phase of her career.

Most dictionaries do not list the principal parts of a regular verb like *enter: enter* (present), *entered* (past and past participle), and *entering* (present participle). But if a verb is irregular—that is, if it forms its past tense in some way other than by adding an *-ed*—the dictionary will usually list three or four principal parts.

race, raced, racing

[Notice that only a *-d* is added to form the past and past participle; therefore the principal parts may be listed in the dictionary.]

drive, drove, driven, driving

[This verb has four listings in the dictionary because it changes form for the past and the past participle as well as the present participle.]

If a verb undergoes no change except for the *-ing* ending of the present participle, the dictionary still lists three principal parts because the verb is not a regular verb.

burst, burst, bursting

Be careful to distinguish between verbs with similar spellings like *sit/set, lie/lay*, and *rise/raise*. Remember that *sit, lie*, and *rise* cannot take objects, but *set, lay*, and *raise* can.

object
While Bonnie *sat* in her favorite chair, John *laid out* several books for her to read and
object
raised the television to a comfortable viewing level.

The books *were set* on a nearby table.

Notice in the second example that the word you expect to be the object of *set*—that is, *books*—is made the subject of the sentence. Thus the subject of the sentence is not acting but is being acted upon. In such a case, the verb is said to be passive.

The verbs *set, lay,* and *raise* can be made passive, but the verbs *sit, lie,* and *rise* cannot because they cannot take objects.

The books were *set* down.   [NOT *sat* down]

The books were *laid* down.   [NOT *lain* down]

The television was *raised*.   [NOT was *risen*]

Of these six difficult verbs, the most troublesome combination is *lie/lay* because the past tense form of *lie* is *lay.*

He *lays* out the books and then *lies* down to rest.

After he had *laid* out the books, he *lay* down to rest.

Be careful to add the *-d* or *-ed* ending to the past and perfect tenses of verbs like *use* and to verbs that end in *-k* or *-t.*

He has us*ed* only ten minutes of his nap time.

She ask*ed* for her copy of A. S. Byatt's *Possession*.

Be careful to spell correctly the principal parts of verbs like *occur, pay,* and *die* that double or change letters.

occur, occu*rr*ed, occu*rr*ing

pay, pa*id*, paying

die, di*ed*, d*y*ing

Subject-verb agreement

The verb must be matched with its subject, not with any word that comes between the subject and verb.

The *combination* of careful planning and knowing birds' habits *ensures* success.

[*Combination*, not *habits*, is the subject.]

Many *birds*, in addition to an occasional bat, *land* in the nets.

[Most writers agree that nouns following expressions like "together with," "in addition to," and "along with" do not affect the number of the subject. Notice that the whole phrase is set off with commas.]

Matching subjects and verbs that end in *-sk* or *-st* requires careful reading. Because of our tendency to leave out certain difficult sounds when speaking, many of us also fail in our writing to add a needed *-s* to a verb or to a subject ending in *-sk* or *-st.*

The *naturalists* study the migratory patterns of birds.

The amateur bird *watcher asks* for the naturalist's help.

Subjects joined by *and* usually take a plural verb.

The *naturalist* and her *assistant handle* the birds carefully.

Exceptions: If the two subjects refer to the same person or thing, or if *each* or *every* comes before the subject, the verb is singular.

The naturalist and leader of this project *directs* the group's efforts.

Every naturalist and every volunteer *recognizes* the importance of the project.

Singular subjects joined by *or, nor, either . . . or,* and *neither . . . nor* usually take a singular verb.

Neither an owl nor a hawk is likely to be caught in the net.

Exception: If one subject is singular and one plural, the verb is matched with the nearer subject, or the sentence is revised to avoid the agreement difficulty.

Neither the hawk nor the nets *survive* such an encounter.

OR

The nets *do* not *survive* the encounter, and neither *does* the hawk.

When the subject follows the verb (as in sentences beginning with *there is* or *there are*), be careful in identifying and matching up subject and verb.

There *is* a *line* of nets across this valley.

There *are thousands* of birds in the grain fields.

Included among the flocks *are hummingbirds* from Costa Rica.

A relative pronoun (*who, whom, which, that*) used as the subject of a clause is singular or plural depending on its antecedent.

Attached to the poles are fabric panels that *funnel* the birds to the nets.

[*Panels,* the antecedent, is plural; therefore, *that* is considered plural.]

Every volunteer who *works* tonight must wear safety glasses.

[*Volunteer,* the antecedent, is singular; therefore, *who* is considered singular.]

Pronoun subjects like *each, one, anybody, everybody, either,* and *neither* usually take singular verbs.

Each of the volunteers *wears* a yellow parka.

Everybody in the woods tonight *needs* to avoid the wire fences.

Pronoun subjects like *all, any, half, most, none,* and *some* may take either a singular or plural verb—the context determines the verb form.

All of the volunteers *attend* the university.

All of their training *comes* in these field trips.

In general, use a singular verb with collective nouns regarded as a unit.

The number of cedar waxwings has decreased each year of the study.

[*The number* is usually regarded as a unit.]

A number of cedar waxwings are seen on campus each fall.

[*A number* usually refers to individuals.]

The *flock is* in the oak tree.

The *majority* of the sightings *were* in the morning.

The verb agrees with the subject, not the subject complement, but it is usually best to avoid disagreement of verb and subject complement by revising the sentence to eliminate the linking verb.

Awkward	My usual *snack* at these field trips *is* fruit juices and salted herring.
	[The verb *is* correctly agrees with the subject *snack,* but the disagreement of verb and subject complement seems awkward to many writers.]
Revised	On field trips I usually snack on fruit juices and salted herring.
	[Replacing the linking verb with an action verb eliminates the problem of disagreement of verb and subject complement.]

Nouns like *news, civics,* and *measles,* even though they have the *s* ending, take singular verbs. Single titles, even if plural in form, are considered singular in number, as are words referred to as words.

The dictionary is the best guide for determining if nouns like these, which have plural endings, take singular verbs.

Economics determines the *duration* of the study.

[The dictionary describes *economics* as singular.]

Feathered Jewels is an important book about hummingbirds.

"Ethnobotanists" is often misspelled. Do you know what it means?

Tense forms

Make the tense forms of verbs and verbals relate logically between subordinate clauses and the main clause and in compound constructions.

When both the main-clause verb and the subordinate-clause verb refer to action occurring now or to action that could occur at any time, use the present tense for both verbs.

When Rucker *studies* art history, he usually *is looking* for inspiration.

[*Is looking*, the progressive form, denotes action that takes place in the past, present, and (probably) future.]

When both the main and the subordinate verbs refer to action that occurred at a definite time in the past, use the past tense for both verbs.

While he *was studying* Impressionist painters, he *discovered* the work of Mary Cassatt.

[*Was studying*, the past progressive form, suggests an action that took place in the past but on a continuing basis.]

When both the main and the subordinate verbs refer to action that continued for some time but was completed before now, use the present perfect tense for both verbs.

He *has stopped* painting landscapes because he *has discovered* the portraits of Cassatt.

Notice that the present tense can be used with the present perfect tense without causing a shift.

Some painters *have stopped* studying the old masters because they *cannot find* inspiration in them.

Some painters *do* not *study* the old masters because they *have found* no inspiration in them.

When the main verb's action occurs at the same time as the verbal's, use the present-tense form of the verbal.

Rucker *continues* to practice his portraits.

Rucker *continued* to practice his portraits.

Continuing to practice his portraits, Rucker *asks* two of his friends to serve as models.

Continuing to practice his portraits, Rucker *asked* two of his friends to serve as models.

On the few occasions when the action of the verbal occurs before the action of the main verb, use the present-perfect tense of the verbal.

Rucker *would like to have painted* landscapes of his family's Mississippi farm.

[Compare "Rucker *wishes he had painted* landscapes."]

Having failed to paint the farm in his youth, he now makes annual pilgrimages south to paint the scenes of his childhood.

[The failure to paint occurred before the annual pilgrimages.]

Be sure that verb tenses in compound predicates are consistent.

He first *photographs* various scenes on the old farm and later *paints* the scenes using the photographs as models.

Mood

In writing, the subjunctive mood is still appropriate in certain constructions.

If Rucker *were asked*, he would fly to the old farm today.

He wishes that he *were* free to return.

The possibility that his brothers will ask him to go requires that he *be prepared* to leave at a moment's notice.

Incorrect shifts in tense or mood

Notice the difference when verb tenses shift unnecessarily in the following examples.

Shift	During the discussion of Andrew's new novel, he *listened* carefully but *said* nothing while his wife *listens* carefully and loudly *applauds* every compliment for the novel.
	[shift from past tense to present tense]
Consistent	During the discussion of Andrew's new novel, he *listened* carefully but *said* nothing while his wife *listened* carefully and loudly *applauded* every compliment for the novel.
Shift	Andrew insists that in his fiction women *be shown* as the strength of the family while men *are* less *committed* to the family.
	[shift from subjunctive mood to indicative mood]
Consistent	Andrew insists that in his fiction women *be shown* as the strength of the family while men *be shown* as less committed to the family.

In writing essays on literature or historical topics, be especially careful to maintain a consistent present tense while retelling a plot or an event.

Shift	Molly *is characterized* as the matriarch of the family who *kept* them together during hard times.
	[shift from present tense to past tense]
Consistent	Molly *is characterized* as the matriarch of the family who *keeps* them together during hard times.

Verb Forms

Name_____ Score _____

DIRECTIONS Use your dictionary to look up the principal parts of the verbs listed below. If the verb is a regular verb—that is, adds an *-ed* for the past and past participle and an *-ing* for the present participle—write *regular* in the blank. But if the verb is not predictable in its tense forms, write *irregular* in the blank and fill in the two or three other parts that your dictionary lists after the present-tense form.

EXAMPLE

think	thought, thinking	irregular
try	tried, trying	regular

1. talk _____ _____

2. grow _____ _____

3. last _____ _____

4. see _____ _____

5. write _____ _____

6. drown _____ _____

7. send _____ _____

8. fly _____ _____

9. argue _____ _____

10. break _____ _____

11. choose _____ _____

12. follow _____ _____

13. kiss _____ _____

14. prepare _____ _____

15. occur _____ _____

16. take _____ _____

17. start _____ _____

18. pass _____ _____

19. add _____ _____

20. carry _____ _____

21. fill _____ _____

22. surpass   _____   _____

23. hit   _____   _____

24. sail   _____   _____

25. fail   _____   _____

Troublesome Verbs

Name_____ **Score** _____

DIRECTIONS In the following sentences cross out the incorrect form or forms of the verb in parentheses and write the correct form in the blank.

EXAMPLE

I (~~use~~, used) to have an office downstairs with a window onto the front yard. _____used_____

1. Now I (sit, set, sits) upstairs with my computer and look out over the fruit trees in the back yard. _____

2. I (like, likes, liked) this vantage point better. _____

3. When I (move, moved) upstairs, I also gained a better view of the many birds in my yard. _____

4. A small flock of juncos (is, are) occupying the feeder today. _____

5. Their tail feathers open and close in scissors fashion as they (hop, hops, hopped) about. _____

6. Each time the feathers flash open, I (glimpse, glimpses, have glimpsed) white feathers against the dominant gray. _____

7. I can see the flash of white only because I (is, am) perched about fifteen feet above them. _____

8. When I noticed that habit in juncos, I (begin, began, begun) to wonder why it exists. _____

9. The flashes of white (makes, make) the bird more visible. _____

10. Juncos feed on the ground, and their gray bodies (blends, blend) easily with their surroundings. _____

11. So why would they evolve this habit that (make, makes) them more visible to hawks flying overhead? _____

12. Hopping among them now is a wren, one of the pair that (nests, nested) in a box in my garden last summer. _____

13. He is silent now, unlike during the summers when his song (fills, filled, has filled) the air. _____

14. He sits atop the box, wreathed by a purple clematis and (tell, tells, told) the world how happy he is to be alive. _____

15. I (leave, left) my window open and enjoy his happiness. _____

16. Occasionally I (sit, sat) in the shade of the birches and read, listening to his song.   _____

17. Wrens (nest, nests) in that box every year, but the babies always slip away unseen.   _____

18. Every year wrens nest in a fern on Victoria's deck, and she (watch, watches, watched) the babies' first flight.   _____

19. James (lock, locks, locked) the side door to his garage to protect the wrens nesting on the lintel above the door.   _____

20. He also (reminds, reminded) the paperboy not to throw the paper against the door.   _____

Verb Forms

Name_____ **Score** _____

DIRECTIONS In the following sentences cross out the incorrect form or forms of the verb in parentheses and write the correct form in the blank.

EXAMPLE

I would like (~~to be~~, to have been) one of the first explorers into California.

to have been

1. Starla wants to be a writer, and she (learned, has learned) to observe the world closely.

_____

2. In 1995 Starla and her family moved here from northern California, and she and I soon (became, have become) best friends.

_____

3. In her old school she (learned, had learned) to write plays.

_____

4. In our first year of friendship Starla (tells, told) me that she wanted to write fiction for children.

_____

5. Although she (has spoken, spoke) fondly of her home in California, she finds more to write about here.

_____

6. I think that may be because she (is matured, has matured) much since moving here.

_____

7. I try (to help, to have helped) her with the writing.

_____

8. Her favorite exercise is (to go, to have gone) "looking," as she calls it.

_____

9. Yesterday we went looking at the hospital courtyard and (saw, seen) something unexpected.

_____

10. We thought we were there (to look, to have looked) at people.

_____

11. As the staff on their lunch breaks came out into the courtyard, we (could hear, could have heard) everyone talking excitedly about "the falcons."

_____

12. We quickly (realize, realized) that they were referring to falcons, the beautiful birds that look like hawks.

_____

13. A doctor sitting near us (says, said, would say) that two falcons were nesting on a ledge on the sixth floor.

_____

14. Starla and I were impressed with the excitement that the
    birds were causing among the hospital staff and decided
    (to convey, to have conveyed) that excitement in our
    writing.   _____

15. We knew that we were lucky (to discover, to have
    discovered) such a wonderful experience in such an
    unexpected place.   _____

Agreement of Subject and Verb

Name_____ **Score** _____

DIRECTIONS In each of the following sentences underline the subject of the verb in parentheses with one line; then match it mentally with the correct verb. Cross out the verb that
does not agree with the subject, and write the verb that does agree in the blank.

EXAMPLE

When birds of prey (nest, ~~nests~~) near humans, excitement always
follows.   *nest*_____

1. A peregrine falcon (is, are) a rare sight.   _____

2. The use of pesticides almost (eliminates, eliminated) falcons
   from this part of the country.   _____

3. Falcons (is, are) at the top of the food chain.   _____

4. They (eat, eats) birds and mice that absorb pesticides from
   the grain they have eaten.   _____

5. The pesticides (affects, affect) the shells of their eggs.   _____

6. Because the fragile eggs (breaks, break) easily, the birds
   do not reproduce at sufficient rates to sustain a population.   _____

7. Government controls on pesticide use (prevents, prevent)
   this natural disaster.   _____

8. Because of the success of this program, Starla and I can sit
   in the hospital courtyard and watch two falcons (visit, visits)
   their nest on a sixth floor ledge.   _____

9. Starla and I (divides, divide) the task of writing about
   the falcons.   _____

10. At first we cannot decide the gender of either bird as he or
    she (land, lands) on the ledge.   _____

11. Everyone else (seem, seems) able to tell the gender easily.   _____

12. Starla (notice, notices) a bird identification chart on a wall.   _____

13. The pictures on the chart (illustrate, illustrates) no differences
    between the male's and female's appearances.   _____

14. Everyone else, we (decides, decide), is guessing.   _____

15. Because they watched the female (sits, sit) on the nest, they
    think they can identify her now.   _____

16. More than twenty people (has, have) gathered at lunch
    break to watch the birds feed their chicks.   _____

17. As either the male or female (land, lands) we try to see
    what he or she is bringing as food.   _____

18. Neither Starla nor I (know, knows) much about the diet of
    falcons.   _____

19. A number of mice (disappears, disappear) into the nest.   _____

20. The hospital staff tells us that the number of pigeons in the
    area also dramatically (decrease, decreases) each day.   _____

Agreement of Subject and Verb

Name_____ Score _____

DIRECTIONS In the following sentences the subjects and verbs are in agreement. Rewrite the sentences, making all italicized singular subjects and verbs plural and all italicized plural subjects and verbs singular. (You will need to drop or add an article—*a, an, the*—before the subject and sometimes change another word or two to make the sentence sound right.) When your answers have been checked, you may want to read the sentences aloud to accustom your ear to the forms that agree with each other.

EXAMPLE

The bird *watcher relies* on a book of photographs of hawks.

Bird watchers rely on a book of photographs of hawks.

1. The *hawk is building* a nest near Central Park in New York.

2. A *photographer sets up* a tripod for his camera.

3. A *truck* for a local television station *parks* across the street.

4. On the evening news the *viewer sees* the nest on a building on 74th Street.

5. One *watcher reminds* us that Woody Allen lives next door.

6. The *hawks seem* as accustomed to crowds as is Woody Allen.

7. *People enjoy* this incursion of the wild into the big city.

8. The *nest envelops* a ledge on the twelfth floor.

9. *All* of us *want* to see the fledglings.

10. But *most* of us *miss* the sight because of work.

UNIT 4 Pronouns

Hodges': chapters 5, 6, 28
Writer's: chapter 21

The form that a noun or pronoun has in a sentence indicates its function, or *case: subjective, objective,* or *possessive.* Nouns usually change their form for only one case—the possessive. (In Unit 8 you will study the ways the apostrophe indicates that change.) Certain pronouns, however, change their form for each case, and you must be aware of the various forms if you want to use these pronouns correctly.

Subjective	Objective	Possessive
I	me	mine
we	us	our OR ours
he, she	him, her	his, her, OR hers
they	them	their OR theirs
who OR whoever	whom OR whomever	whose

A pronoun has no real meaning of its own; rather, it depends on its antecedent, the word it refers to, for its meaning. If a pronoun does not refer clearly and logically to another word, then your reader will not know what the pronoun means. And if a pronoun refers broadly to the general idea of the preceding sentence or sentences, the reader may have to reread a part or parts of the earlier material to try to determine the meaning of the pronoun.

They claim that *their* history of Jefferson Springs is true. *They* say *this* because of *their* interviews with former Jefferson Springs residents.

There are three main ways to correct an unclear reference of a pronoun: (1) rewrite the sentence or sentences to eliminate the pronoun; (2) provide a clear antecedent for the pronoun to refer to; or (3) substitute a noun for the pronoun or, as in the case of *this,* add a noun, making the pronoun an adjective.

The students in Professor Kates' class claim that their history of Jefferson Springs is true. *They* make *this claim* because *they* interviewed several former Jefferson Springs residents.

[Note in the second sentence that *this* has become an adjective modifying the noun *claim.*]

Pronoun-antecedent agreement

Use a singular pronoun to refer to such antecedents as *each, everyone, nobody, one, a person, a woman,* and *a man.*

Each of the students developed *her* section of the history.

Today writers make every effort to avoid sexism in the use of personal pronouns. Whereas writers once wrote, "Each of us should do his best," they now try to avoid using the masculine pronoun to refer to both men and women. To avoid sexism, some writers give both masculine and feminine pronoun references.

Each of us developed *his* or *her* section.

Each of us developed *his/her* section

[Compare "Each of us developed a section."]

Other writers prefer to use *one's* in place of his or her.

One should write *one's* own section.

Perhaps the easiest way to avoid sexism is to use plural pronouns and antecedents unless a feminine or a masculine pronoun is clearly called for.

All of them wrote *their* sections.

All of us wrote *our* sections.
                        BUT
Each of the women wrote *her* section.

A plural pronoun is used to refer to two or more antecedents joined by *and;* a singular pronoun is used to refer to two or more antecedents joined by *or* or *nor.*

Sarah and Tracey have presented *their* reports on Jefferson Springs tower.

Neither Sarah *nor* Tracey has completed *her* final draft.

If it is necessary to have one singular and one plural antecedent, make the pronoun agree with the closer antecedent.

Neither Sarah nor her *friends* know when *their* final drafts will be finished.

Again, as with the verb, it is sometimes best to rephrase to avoid the pronoun agreement difficulty.

Tracey does not know when *her* draft will be finished, nor do her friends know when *theirs* will be finished.

Use either a singular or a plural pronoun to refer to a collective noun like *team, staff,* or *group,* depending on whether the noun is considered a unit or a group of individuals.

The city *council* in my hometown is offering *its* support for the students' research on Jefferson Springs.

[*Council* is acting as a unit. Notice that both the pronoun and the verb must be the same number.]

The *council* are discussing *their* votes at a meeting tonight.

[The individuals in the council are referred to; thus both the pronoun and the verb are plural.]

When the collective noun is considered plural, as *council* is in the preceding example, many writers prefer to use *members of the council* rather than a noun that looks singular.

The *members of the council* are voting to fund the students' field trips.

The pronoun that refers to such antecedents as *all, most, half, none,* and *some* is usually plural, but in a few contexts it can be singular.

All of them took *their* turns.

Most of the students said *they* had never used a tape recorder in *their* research.

Most of their preparation proved *itself* worthwhile.

Pronoun reference

Avoid unclear reference.

Ambiguous	Wallace told Bart that he was innately aggressive.
Clear	Wallace told Bart, "You are innately aggressive."
	OR
	Wallace told Bart, "I am innately aggressive."

Avoid remote or obscure reference. A pronoun that is located too far from its antecedent, with too many intervening nouns, will not have a clear meaning; nor will a pronoun that refers to an antecedent in the possessive case.

Remote	In the distance Jennifer can see the horses in the tree line. She walks along the river, noticing the occasional fossil exposed by the low water and picking up several arrowheads. The trees obscure *their* outlines.
	[Readers might think that *their* refers to arrowheads.]
Clear	In the distance Jennifer can see the *horses, their* outlines obscured in the tree line. She walks along the river, noticing the occasional fossil exposed by the low water and picking up several arrowheads.
Obscure	When her father's car drove up, Jennifer was glad to see *him*.
	[*Him* illogically refers to *car*.]

Clear   When her *father* drove up in his car, Jennifer was glad to see *him*.

                         [*Him* logically refers to *father.*]

In general, avoid broad reference. Pronouns such as *this, it, that, which,* and *such* may sometimes be used effectively to refer to the general idea of a preceding sentence, or even of a preceding paragraph. But such broad reference is easily misused and should generally be avoided. Make sure that each pronoun you use has a clear reference.

Broad   Jennifer's passion is horses, so she used *this* as the focal
                         point of her Jefferson Springs project.

Clear   Jennifer's passion is horses, so she researched the role of
                         horses in the history of Jefferson Springs.

Avoid using *it* in two ways in the same sentence. Avoid using the pronouns *it* and *you* awkwardly.

Confusing   Although *it* was time-consuming to read the article before
                         class, we did read *it*.

                         [The first *it* is an expletive, the second *it* refers to article.]

Clear   Although reading the *article* before class was time-
                         consuming, we did read *it*.

Awkward   In the article "The History of a Small Town," *it* discusses how
                         to conduct research into local history.

                         [The pronoun *it* refers clumsily to *article.*]

Clear   The article "The History of a Small Town," discusses how to
                         conduct research into local history.

Awkward   *One* may read this article for a basic introduction to the
                         process. *You* may also be surprised that the author is
                         Professor Kates.

Clear   *One* may read this article for a basic introduction to the
                         process. *One* may also be surprised that the author is
                         Professor Kates.

Note: Some grammarians assert that *you* is both natural and correct as long as the writer does not shift person in the sentence or the paragraph; other grammarians argue that *you* should be avoided in formal composition. Before using *you* in your writing, discuss the usage with your instructor.

Pronoun case (subjective, objective, and possessive)

A gerund is a verbal that ends in *-ing* and is used as a noun. The possessive case is used before a gerund, which acts as a noun, but not before a participle, which also sometimes has an *-ing* ending but acts as an adjective.

Jennifer's parents grew weary of *her* complaining that she had nothing new to wear.

[*Complaining* is a gerund and functions as the object of the preposition *of.*]

That afternoon they found *her* admiring her new tattoo.

[*Admiring* is a participle, an adjective modifying *her.*]

Pronouns use the objective form for the subject or object of an infinitive.

Professor Kates wanted Jennifer and *me* to present the first report.

[subject of the infinitive *to present*]

I liked to help Jennifer and *him*.   [object of the infinitive *to help*]

Pronouns use the subjective case for a subject complement.

She and *I* work well together.

The leader is *she*.

[Using a pronoun as a complement can seem awkward. If that is so, write "She is the leader."]

Pronouns in compound constructions

When you are using a single pronoun, you may have no difficulty choosing the right case.

I conducted the interview with *her.*

But when other pronouns or nouns are added, you may become confused about case and write, "Him and me attended the play with Ted and she." If you tend to make such errors in case, think of the function each pronoun would have if it were used in a separate sentence.

He sat outside.   [NOT *Him* sat outside.]

I sat outside.   [NOT *Me* sat outside.]

I sat outside with *her*.   [NOT I sat outside with *she.*]

Then you will be more likely to write the correct case forms:

He and *I* taped an interview with Gaylord and *her.*

Who vs. whom

If you examine the use of a pronoun in its own clause, you can determine its case.

Use *who* or *whoever* as the subject of a clause. When a sentence has only one clause, the function of a pronoun may seem clear to you.

Who is conducting these interviews?   [*Who* is the subject of the verb *is conducting.*]

Whoever will be our first guest.

But when another clause is added, you must be careful to determine the pronoun's use in its own clause.

I know *who* is conducting the interviews.

[Although *who* introduces a clause that acts as the direct object of the verb *know,* in its own clause *who* is the subject of the verb *is conducting.*]

In formal writing use *whom* for all objects.

The woman *whom* we met last night is not here.   [object of the verb *met*]

The woman to *whom* we gave the video tape is not here tonight.

[object of the preposition *to*]

Whom should we ask about the video tape?   [object of the verb *ask*]

Case of Pronouns

Name_____ **Score** _____

DIRECTIONS In the following sentences cross out the incorrect case form or forms in parentheses and write the correct form in the blank.

EXAMPLE

My parents had helped to found my home town and had taught
(me, ~~myself~~) some of the history.   *me*_____

1. I knew that my parents formed one of the five couples
   (who, whom) had started the community.   _____

2. My father had lived in a commune (who, whose) members
   encouraged him to start a similar experiment elsewhere.   _____

3. For (they, them) knew that he could not be happy in a
   traditional community.   _____

4. My parents told my sisters and (I, me) to learn a lesson from
   their experiences.   _____

5. The first lesson for (us, we) to learn was to be careful in
   choosing the people to share our dreams.   _____

6. Then they told us about the other couples (who, whom) they
   convinced to participate in their dream.   _____

7. (Me, My) going to college affected how I thought about my
   personal history.   _____

8. My history teacher and (me, I) had similar childhoods.   _____

9. Like (me, myself) she grew up in a very small town.   _____

10. My community, however, was created by people to (who, whom)
    a utopia seemed a practical idea.   _____

11. My teacher's family founded a community near a new
    railroad, and in (them, their) doing so they ensured a
    prosperous life for the whole family.   _____

12. The families in my community intended to escape commerce
    and competition for money. They taught my sisters and (I, me)
    to depend on the land for our sustenance.   _____

13. By (them, their) not permitting us to mingle with outsiders,
    they thought they could ensure that we would grow up
    unaffected by the outside world.   _____

14. Neither my sisters nor (me, I) abided by their wishes.   _____

15. By the time we were ten years old, we had convinced them to permit (us, we) to go to school in the closest town and to stop being home schooled.   _____

Pronoun Case and Agreement

Name _____   Score _____

DIRECTIONS In the following sentences cross out the incorrect case form or forms in parentheses and write the correct form in the blank.

EXAMPLE

The two women (~~who~~, whom) this plaque honors are the true
founders of this small community.   *whom* _____

1. A community also honors itself when it eagerly gives credit
   to individuals (who, whom) have been its leaders.   _____

2. Each of the Young sisters made a name for (herself, themselves)
   within the community.   _____

3. Many of you (who, whom) play the piano learned the skill
   from Betty Young.   _____

4. To you and (I, me) the long walk to her front door every
   Tuesday afternoon after school might have seemed daunting.   _____

5. A piano student had to give (their, his, her) best at
   each practice.   _____

6. Of course, the sisters also lived in the old log cabin all of
   their lives. (Them, Their) being in such an isolated and
   picturesque setting affected all of us.   _____

7. Betty Young used that setting when she taught you and
   (I, me) piano lessons.   _____

8. All of us (who, whom) she taught have sat on the porch and
   listened to the river below.   _____

9. At recitals she would remind us to think of the river sounds
   to calm our nerves. (Who, Whom) among you remembers that
   sound even now?   _____

10. Louise Young taught us similar lessons when she taught
    us Latin. To (who, whom) in this gathering did she teach Latin?   _____

11. Her students learned for (theirselves, themselves) how to study
    every day.   _____

12. Those of us (who, whom) were raised on television thought
    Latin was a dead language.   _____

13. But she taught (you and I, you and me) that Latin lives
    through its influence on the English language.   _____

14. I was one of those students (who, whom) Ms. Young
     powerfully influenced.   _____

15. I learned from her how to work every day to accomplish a task.
     For (me, my) to have made it through college is a testament
     to her influence.   _____

Reference of Pronouns   Exercise 4-3

Name_____   **Score** _____

DIRECTIONS In the following sentences write a V above each pronoun whose reference is
vague or awkward and write that pronoun in the blank. Then revise the sentence or sentences to clarify the meaning. Not all sentences require correction.

EXAMPLE

    It is interesting to read Watson's essay because it teaches us
about our community.   _____*it*_____

*Watson's essay interests us because it teaches us
about our community.*

1. In Watson's article it explains how she learned to weave
   from Betty Young.   _____

2. Watson's parents did not encourage her because this seemed
   inappropriate to them.   _____

3. Some of her friends believed that Ms. Young would not teach it
   to her.   _____

4. Bennett had imagined finding a wise teacher skilled in all
   aspects of the craft, which would be the ideal arrangement
   for her.   _____

5. But it was proving impossible to find a person to teach it.   _____

6. Betty Young was a master weaver, and she used this to teach
   Watson.   _____

7. Betty taught her to make dyes from plants and yarn from wool.
   Watson learned it eagerly.   _____

8. It became important for Watson to apply all of her skills, so she
   began it on her new cedar loom.   _____

9. Local custom would have her weave a pattern of stripes which
   seemed to her to be too little of a challenge.   _____

10. She decided to use all of her colors of yarn and all of her designing skills to create a sampler. Only in a sampler could she display all of them.   _____

11. During this weaving she made a mistake. In it she wove the image of a star.   _____

12. It is bad luck to weave a falling star image, but she corrected it by weaving in a hand about to catch the falling star.   _____

UNIT 5

Modifiers

Hodges': chapters 4, 25
Writer's: chapter 20

Both adjectives and adverbs function as modifiers; that is, they make the meaning of the words they refer to more exact. In the examples below, notice that the meaning becomes clearer and more detailed as modifiers are added (adjectives are in boldface, adverbs in italics).

> An interview with her mother provided a topic for her project.

> An **extended** interview with her **ill** mother provided a **gripping** topic for her **final research** project.

> An **extended** interview with her **recently ill** mother *quickly* provided a *surprisingly* **gripping** topic for her **final research** project.

The adjective *extended* modifies the noun subject *interview;* the adjectives *ill* modify *mother,* the object of a preposition; the adjective *gripping* modifies the noun complement *topic;* and the adjectives *final* and *research* modify *project,* the object of a preposition. Typically, adjectives modify nouns and sometimes pronouns. The adverbs—*recently, quickly,* and *surprisingly*—modify the adjective *ill,* the verb *provided,* and the adjective *gripping.* Typically, adverbs modify verbs and modifiers (both adjectives and adverbs).

A modern dictionary will show you the current usage of adjective and adverb modifiers. But here are a few guidelines.

Adverbs

Adverbs modify verbs, adjectives, and other adverbs.

> She *often* draws ideas from personal experience.

> [*Often* modifies the verb *draws.*]

> She *often* uses interviews to develop *unusually* challenging themes.

> [*Often* modifies the verb *uses; unusually* modifies the adjective *challenging.*]

The interviews *almost always* teach her new points of view.

[*Always* modifies the verb *teach*; *almost* modifies the adverb *always*.]

Adjectives

Adjectives, like nouns, are used as complements after linking verbs such as *be, appear, become, feel, look, seem, smell,* and *taste*. Such adjective complements refer to the subjects of their clauses.

Her interviews seem *conversational* and *spontaneous,* but they actually are *planned* and *structured*.

[*Conversational* and *spontaneous* refer to *interviews,* the subject of the first main clause; *planned* and *structured* refer to *they,* the subject of the second main clause.]

She believes that every interview is *successful*.

[*Successful* refers to *interview,* the subject of the subordinate clause.]

Painful were her first interviews.

[For emphasis, the complement, *painful,* comes before but still refers to the subject, *interviews.*]

A sensory verb like *feel, taste,* or *look* is followed by an adverb instead of an adjective when the modifier refers to the verb.

She looked *uncomfortably* at her mother.

[Compare "She looked *uncomfortable*," in which *uncomfortable,* an adjective complement, modifies the subject, *she.*]

A linking verb followed by an adjective complement may also be modified by one or more adverbs, coming either before or after the verb.

The interviewer *suddenly* seemed happy *yesterday*.

[Both adverbs modify *seemed.* The adjective *happy* modifies the subject *interviewer.*]

Many adjectives and adverbs change form to indicate degree of comparison. The comparative degree (a comparison of two things) is usually formed by adding *-er* to the modifier or by putting *more* or *less* before the modifier. The superlative degree (a comparison of three or more things) is formed by adding *-est* to the modifier or by putting the word *most* or *least* before the modifier. Some desk dictionaries show the *-er* and *-est* endings for adjectives and adverbs that form their comparative and superlative degrees in this way (for example, *old, older, oldest*). Most dictionaries show the changes for highly irregular modifiers (for example, *good, better, best*). As a rule of thumb, most one-syllable adjectives and most two-syllable adjectives ending in a vowel sound (*tidy, narrow*) form the comparative with *-er* and the superlative with *-est*. Most adjectives of two or more syllables and most adverbs form the comparative by adding the word *more* (*less*) and the superlative by adding the word *most* (*least*).

Nonstandard	The dialog seemed more better written.
	[The -er shows the comparative degree; *more* is superfluous.]
Standard	The dialog seemed better written.
Nonstandard	She was the better prepared of the interviewers.
	[*Better* is used to compare only two things.]
Standard	She was the best prepared of all the interviewers.

Note: Current usage, however illogical it may seem, accepts comparisons of many adjectives or adverbs with absolute meanings, such as "a *more perfect* society," "the *deadest* campus," and "*less completely* exhausted." But many writers make an exception of *unique*—using "*more nearly* unique" rather than "*more unique*." They consider *unique* an absolute adjective—one without degrees of comparison.

We correctly use many nouns as modifiers of other nouns—*soap* opera, *book* club, *menu* item—because there are no suitable adjective forms available. But when adjective forms are available, you should avoid awkward noun substitutes.

Awkward	Education television presented an interview with Boris Yeltsin.
Better	*Educational* television presented an interview with Boris Yeltsin.

The term *double negative* refers to the use of two negatives to express a single negation. A single rather than a double negative is correct.

Nonstandard	He did not have no memory of being interviewed.
	[double negative: *not* and *no*]
Standard	He did not have a memory of being interviewed.
	[single negative: *not*]
	OR
	He had no memory of being interviewed.
	[single negative: *no*]

Another redundant construction occurs when a negative such as *not, nothing,* or *without* is combined with *hardly, barely,* or *scarcely.*

Nonstandard	She couldn't hardly stop talking during the interview.
Standard	She could hardly stop talking during the interview.
Nonstandard	She spoke easily, without hardly any prompting.
Standard	She spoke easily, with hardly any prompting.

Placement of modifiers

An adverb clause can usually be moved to various places in a sentence without affecting the meaning or clarity of the sentence.

After Bill Moyers interviewed Joseph Campbell, the audience asked several questions.

The audience asked several questions *after Bill Moyers interviewed Joseph Campbell.*

The movement of the adverb clause affects the punctuation of the sentence and the part of the sentence to be emphasized. But the sentence has the same meaning and that meaning is clear whether the adverb clause is an introductory, interrupting, or concluding addition.

Other sentence parts may not be moved around so easily, as the following discussions of various modifiers will show.

In standard written English, adverbs such as *almost, only, just, hardly, nearly,* and *merely* are usually placed immediately before the words they modify.

Misplaced	Campbell nearly spoke three hours without using notes.
Better	Campbell spoke nearly three hours without using notes.
Misplaced	His latest book only deals with Hindu mythology.
Better	His latest book deals only with Hindu mythology.

Place prepositional phrases to indicate clearly the words that they modify.

Misplaced	Moyers' questions enabled Campbell to explain the thesis of his latest book *about religion.*
Clear	Moyers' questions *about religion* enabled Campbell to explain the thesis of his latest book.

As long as no awkwardness results, a prepositional phrase can be moved to different places in a sentence for variety.

Judy Cox completely changed, *after Campbell's interview*, her thesis topic.

[The *after* phrase modifies *changed.*]

After Campbell's interview, Judy Cox completely changed her thesis topic.

Judy Cox completely changed her thesis topic *after Campbell's interview.*

Unlike the adverb clause discussed at the beginning of this section, an adjective clause cannot be moved around freely in a sentence without changing the meaning or causing a lack of clarity.

Clear	Changing the structure of her essay, *which was in three parts*, involved adding a fourth section.
Unclear	Changing, *which was in three parts*, the structure of her essay involved adding a fourth section.
	[The placement of the *which* clause now suggests that *changing was in three parts.*]
Unclear	Changing the structure of her essay involved adding a fourth section, *which was in three parts.*
	[Here the *which* clause seems to modify *section.*]

For the sentence to make sense, the adjective clause must be placed immediately after the word it modifies. Other examples include:

Clear	Darlene, *who has asked for Judy's help with an essay*, is writing on Joseph Campbell.
Misplaced	Darlene is writing on Joseph Campbell *who has asked for Judy's help with an essay.*
Misplaced	A student seems likely to succeed as a writer *who is willing to ask for help.*
Clear	A student *who is willing to ask for help* seems likely to succeed as a writer.

Avoid "squinting" constructions—modifiers that may refer to either a preceding or a following word.

Squinting	Karen was asked *on May 21, 2000,* to read her essay before the entire class.
	[The adverbial phrase can modify either *was asked* or *to read.*]
Clear	Karen was asked to read her essay before the entire class *on May 21, 2000.*
	OR
	Karen was asked to read her essay *on May 21, 2000,* before the entire class.

The parts of the sentence base should not be awkwardly separated, nor should an infinitive be awkwardly split.

Awkward	Debbie's essay, *after it was read before the class and at the Honors' Lyceum,* **generated** a great deal of interest in Joseph Campbell.
	[The verb is awkwardly separated from its subject.]
Better	*After it was read before the class and before the Honors' Lyceum,* Debbie's essay **generated** a great deal of interest in Joseph Campbell.
Awkward	Debbie intends **to,** *after it has been completely revised,* **submit** the paper for publication.
	[The prepositional phrase awkwardly splits the infinitive *to submit.*]
Better	*After it has been completely revised,* Debbie intends **to submit** the paper for publication.

Although the awkward splitting of an infinitive should be avoided, sometimes an infinitive split by a single modifier is acceptable and sounds natural.

Judy was able to *quickly* place two of her poems in *Ploughshares.*

Dangling modifiers

Dangling modifiers are most often dangling verbal phrases that do not refer clearly and logically to a word or phrase in the sentence base. To correct a dangling modifier, either rearrange the words in the sentence base so that the modifier clearly refers to the right word, or add the missing words that will make the modifier clear and logical.

Dangling	*Written while she was in the creative writing class,* Debbie narrated her first experiences as a grandmother.
	[The verbal phrase illogically modifies *Debbie.*]
Clear	Written while she was in the creative writing class, Debbie's stories narrated her first experiences as a grandmother.
	[The verbal phrase logically modifies *stories.*]
Dangling	*Thinking about the new life that she holds in her hands,* the stories express the awe she feels at her twin grandsons' birth.
	[The verbal phrase illogically modifies *stories.*]
Clear	*Thinking about the new life that she holds in her hands,* Debbie expresses the awe she feels at the birth of her twin grandsons.
	[The verbal phrase logically modifies *Debbie.*]

OR

Debbie, *thinking about the new life that she holds in her hands,* expresses the awe she feels at the birth of her twin grandsons.

Adjectives and Adverbs

Name_____ **Score** _____

DIRECTIONS In each of the following sentences cross out the incorrect modifier within the parentheses and write in the blank the choice that represents standard usage. Underline the word or words being modified by the modifier you chose. (Consult your dictionary if you are in doubt about the proper form of the comparative or superlative degree of an adjective or adverb.)

EXAMPLE

Jeff <u>writes</u> (sensitively, ~~sensitive~~) about his ancestors.   *sensitively*

1. He lives in a (historical, historically) region known for supporting several utopian communities. _____

2. The (more, most) famous of the utopian communities was formed by Shakers. _____

3. The Shaker community was built in a (relative, relatively) isolated part of his county. _____

4. Jeff's mother works two days a week at the Shaker community as a guide, and she can describe Shaker furniture (perfect, perfectly). _____

5. In the middle of the nineteenth century more than 4,000 converts were (active, actively) as Shakers. _____

6. Shakers accepted a life of (complete, completely) celibacy, so they depended on converts to sustain their faith. _____

7. The (austere, austerely) lives of the Shakers helped them strive for perfection. _____

8. The young and (eager, eagerly) Ann Lee joined a group of religious reformers in 1780. _____

9. Like many other people of her time, she was (desperate, desperately) to achieve perfection on earth. _____

10. She joined the Shaking Quakers, a name given to them because they trembled when possessed by (religious, religiously) ecstasy. _____

11. Tormented by the loss of her four children but (hopeful, hopefully) of some comfort, Ann Lee joined the Quakers. _____

12. A vision convinced her that celibacy was necessary for an (innocent, innocently) existence. _____

13. When she came to America in 1774, she (quick, quickly) established the Shaker sect. _____

Below, make the choices that avoid double negatives.

14. I did not know (nothing, anything) about Shakers until
    I took this class.   _____

15. After I moved to Kentucky, I (could, could not) hardly
    ignore the Shaker history.   _____

16. Because my mother wants me to learn about Ann Lee,
    I never expect to have (any, no) relief from studying her. _____

17. My teacher left hardly (anything, nothing) to chance by
    assigning me the Shakers as a research topic.   _____

18. My best resource is my aunt who has not read (any, no)
    literature about the Shakers but knows their local history. _____

Adjectives and Adverbs

Name_____ **Score** _____

DIRECTIONS While preserving the meaning, rewrite each of the following sentences, changing the italicized adjective to an adverb and the italicized noun to a verb or an adjective, as
in the example below. (You will have to make a few other changes in the sentence in addition to changing the italicized words.)

EXAMPLE

During English class our teacher demonstrated an *unexpected enthusiasm* for revision.

During English class our teacher became unexpectedly enthusiastic about revision.

1. Dr. Barnett devised an *ingenious plan* for teaching revision.

2. The conciseness of a one-act play is a *great delight* to Dr. Barnett.

3. She extended an *excited invitation* to the class to revise their essays into one-act plays.

4. We felt *great relief* that she was not giving us a traditional revision assignment.

5. My group's one-act play on Ann Lee and the Shakers made *a strong impression* on the
class.

Placement of Modifiers

Name_____ **Score** _____

DIRECTIONS Below each of the following sentences is a word, phrase, or clause that, if insert-ed correctly in the sentence, could serve as a clear and logical modifier. Write *1* in the blank if the modifier can be inserted in only one place in the sentence and *2* if it can be inserted in two or more places. Then write the sentence with the modifier placed in all the positions where it will not cause an unclear or awkward sentence.

EXAMPLE

Sam Stewart's first book *Southern Utopias* describes an automobile journey across the south.
which was published in 1983 _____*1*_____

Sam Stewart's first book Southern Utopias, which was published in 1983, describes an automobile journey across the south.

1. The essays discuss Stewart's latest book.
   that were written in my Advanced Writing class _____

2. The students brought them to the library.
   where they were to make copies for everyone _____

3. These papers count as twenty-five percent of the course grade.
   according to the syllabus _____

4. Tricia will read her paper to the class.
   after we have completed discussion of *Southern Utopias* _____

5. The latest draft of her paper lies on my desk.
   awaiting revision _____

6. We will submit it next fall to the Popular Culture Association.
   if she is happy with the revision _____

7. One paper has already been accepted for the meeting.
   that Jamal submitted _____

8. We will be pleased to have several papers accepted.
   however _____

Placement of Modifiers

Name_____ **Score** _____

DIRECTIONS Rewrite each of the following sentence bases so that the modifier that follows is clearly and logically related to a word or phrase in the sentence base. Or expand the modifier so that it is clear by itself when it is attached to the sentence base. (Include examples of both methods in your answers.) Be sure to capitalize and to punctuate the modifier correctly when you attach it to the sentence base.

EXAMPLE

Peggy decided to write several drafts of this essay.
  remembering her instructor's reaction to her last essay

Remembering her instructor's reaction to her last essay, Peggy decided to write several drafts of this essay.

1. This essay examines Sam Stewart's *Southern Utopias*.
    taking a very contemporary perspective

2. Peggy had been thinking about the term "utopia."
    used to describe a perfect community

3. Peggy had lived near Oak Ridge, Tennessee, for many years.
    an experimental scientific community

4. She had realized that it also was an experiment in utopian ideals.
    having thought about its goals

5. Reading Stewart's book reminded her of experiences in Oak Ridge.
    that showed the community's shared goals

6. She wanted to learn about other utopias.
    especially their explicit goals

7. Stewart's book provided an itinerary.
    indicating a route she could follow

8. She decided to visit Pleasant Hill, Kentucky.
   once a Shaker community

9. In her paper Peggy is focusing on utopian goals.
   common to different utopian experiments

10. Something in this project has affected her deeply.
    seeing people's lives shaped by their dreams

PART 2

Punctuation and Other Mechanics of Writing

UNIT 6

Comma

Hodges': chapters 12, 13
Writer's: chapter 31

Of all the marks of punctuation, the most frequently used is the comma. Commas have four main uses:

a to follow a main clause that is linked to another main clause by a coordinate conjunction (*and, but, or, nor, for, so, yet*);
b to follow certain introductory elements
c to separate items in a series, including coordinate (equal in rank) adjectives;
d to set off nonrestrictive, parenthetical, and miscellaneous elements.

After introductory elements in a sentence (words, phrases, dependent clauses)

A comma usually follows adverb clauses that precede main clauses. A comma often follows introductory phrases (especially adverb phrases) and transitional expressions. A comma follows an introductory interjection or an introductory *yes* or *no*.

When an adverb clause precedes the main clause, it is usually followed by a main clause.

Although her father was a struggling immigrant, he still found resources to help his family.

There is usually no comma before the adverb clause when it follows the main clause.

He supported a niece *while she attended college.*

But if the adverb clause at the end begins with *although,* a comma is normally used.

Ruth viewed her father as the strongest person in her world, *although she also recognized his frail health.*

Some writers omit the comma after the introductory adverb clause when the clause is very short or when it has the same subject as the main clause, but there is nothing wrong with including the comma.

Because he worked long hours he neglected his health.

OR

Because he worked long hours, he neglected his health.

In general, do not use a comma before an adverbial clause at the end of a sentence.

Most of us head for the computer lab , when we have to write a paper. [If the *when* clause came at the beginning of the sentence as an introductory addition, it would be followed by a comma.]

A comma usually follows an introductory verbal phrase and may follow an introductory prepositional phrase.

Working long hours and not eating properly, we often become ill.

[introductory verbal phrase]

In this course and in two other courses, I have nine papers to write.

[introductory prepositional phrase]

The comma is often omitted after prepositional phrases if no misreading could result.

In 1998 we published an essay in *Collage.*

Before the deadline we met at the Red Rose Coffee House.

A comma follows an introductory transitional expression, an interjection, and sometimes a single-word modifier.

To be thorough, we researched our topic in the on-line catalog.

Yes, we also went to the library.

Unfocused, the on-line search could have taken too much time.

Certainly, we meant to include all local writers in the search.

[Writers may or may not use a comma after an introductory word like *yet, thus,* and *certainly,* depending on how closely they feel the word is related to the rest of the sentence. If they see the word as functioning primarily for transition, they use a comma; if they see it primarily as an adverb, closely related to the verb, they do not use a comma.]

Before a coordinating conjunction

A comma follows a main clause that is linked to another main clause by a coordinating conjunction: *and, but, or, nor, for, so,* or *yet.*

Sylvia was a chemistry major in college, and she planned to enter medical school.

When the two main clauses are linked by a coordinating conjunction, a compound sentence results.

PATTERN   MAIN CLAUSE, coordinating conjunction MAIN CLAUSE.

Sylvia was a chemistry major in college, and she planned to enter medical school.

The semicolon may also be used when the two main clauses that are linked by a coordinating conjunction contain other commas.

Although neither of her parents had a college education, they planned for their children to go to college; and they worked long hours to fulfill that dream.

[Remember that the addition of another main clause, rather than the presence of the coordinating conjunction, is the reason for the punctuation mark.]

Notice in the following examples that a comma is used before a coordinating conjunction only when the conjunction links two main clauses.

Two Verb Phrases	Sylvia's parents emigrated from Cambodia and settled in a city with a small Asian population.
Two Subordinate Clauses	Because they came to America with few resources and because they wished to build a better life for their children, Sylvia's parents worked long hours in their restaurant.
Two Main Clauses	We can appreciate the immigrant spirit, and we can recognize it as one of the strengths of this country.

Between items in a series

Commas are used between items in a series and between coordinate adjectives. A series is a succession of three or more parallel elements.

Use commas between three or more items in a series.

PATTERN   1, 2, and 3

         OR

PATTERN   1, 2, 3

For the first ten minutes we discussed the test, the grades, and the next assignment.

Karen decided to do her senior thesis on Maxine Kingston because she wanted to study a contemporary writer, because she already had read *Woman Warrior,* and because she had seen a PBS special on Kingston.

Karen also decided to take her oral exam over three writers who champion minorities: Leslie Silko, Zora Neal Hurston, and Richard Wright.

The comma before the *and* may be omitted only if there is no difficulty reading the series or if the two items should be regarded as one unit.

1 2   3
Dr. Collier marked pages 4, 7, and 9 of Karen's thesis as needing revision.

[Without the last comma the series remains clear: Professor Collier marked pages 4, 7, and 9 of Karen's thesis as needing revision.]

1   2   3
Karen had marked the text with numbers, letters, and blue and white sticky notes.

[*Blue* and *white* refers as a unit to *notes;* thus there is no comma before the last and.]

All the commas are normally omitted when a coordinating conjunction is used between each item in the series.

1   2   3
Some students ignore or misread or even refuse to believe the remarks that their

teachers put on their papers.

Semicolons may be used between the items in the series if the items themselves contain commas or if the items are main clauses.

1
Karen's revision process involves three steps: first, she sets a draft aside for a few
2
days; second, she reads the draft carefully for unclear language, underdeveloped
3
passages, and errors; third, she passes the corrected draft to Professor Collier for her

approval or corrections.

Caution: Remember that no comma is used when only two items are linked by a conjunction.

Putting the draft aside and *working on something else* enables her to become objective about the draft.

Use commas between coordinate adjectives that are not linked by a coordinating conjunction.
If the adjectives are coordinate, you can reverse their order or insert *and* or *or* between them without loss of sense.

a   b   a   b
Karen's longest, most successful chapter discusses the difficult, extremely intricate

symbolism in *Tripmaster Monkey.*

a   b   a
Karen's most successful and longest chapter discusses the extremely intricate and
b
difficult symbolism in *Tripmaster Monkey.*

Caution: Adjectives that are not coordinate take no commas between them.

The *brief concluding* chapter suggests other approaches to Kingston's work that Karen hopes to explore.

[You would not say "brief and concluding chapter."]

Coordinate Adejctives: *recurring, insightful* allusions

[You may say "*insightful, recurring* allusions" or "*recurring* and *insightful* allusions."]

Adjectives That Are Not Coordinate: *famous lyric* poem and *longest first* sentence

[You would not say "*famous* and *lyric* poem" or "*first longest* sentence."]

With nonrestrictive or parenthetical elements

Commas set off (1) nonrestrictive clauses and phrases, (2) parenthetical elements such as transitional expressions, and (3) items in dates and addresses.

A comma follows a parenthetical or nonrestrictive addition that comes before the basic sentence pattern.

One of the best books in recent years by an American writer, Legacies: A Chinese Mosaic traces the author's Chinese heritage.

If the parenthetical or nonrestrictive addition comes after the basic sentence, a comma precedes it.

Legacies: A Chinese Mosaic tells the story of Bette Bao Lord, *a best-selling American author.*

The most common position for the parenthetical or nonrestrictive addition is in the middle of the sentence, where one comma precedes it and another comma follows it.

In the second chapter, "*Black Armbands, Red Armbands,*" Lord begins to tell the stories of many who resisted communist rule.

Many of the people closest to her, *including members of her family,* had been members of the Red Guard.

Commas set off nonrestrictive clauses and phrases. Restrictive clauses and phrases are not set off.

A restrictive clause or phrase limits the meaning of the word to which it refers.

The magazine *that published our essay* is called *Collage.*

[The *that* clause limits the meaning of the word *magazine.* Note that the relative pronoun *that* always introduces a relative clause.]

Anyone *reading this magazine* is impressed with the creative writing.

[The verbal phrase *reading this magazine* limits the meaning of the word *anyone.*]

A nonrestrictive clause or phrase does not limit the meaning of the word it refers to; rather, it adds information about a word that is already clearly limited in meaning. The nonrestrictive clause or phrase is set off with commas.

"An American in Cambodia," taken from the magazine *Collage,* explores Francine's return to her homeland.

[The verbal phrase *taken from the magazine Collage* adds further information about the subject "An American in Cambodia."]

Adam Matzger, *who is a freelance writer living in Beijing,* is familiar with Francine and with her visit to Cambodia.

[The *who* clause adds information about *Adam Matzger.*]

Of course, not all adjective clauses and phrases are as obviously restrictive or non-restrictive as the ones used in the preceding examples. Many times you can determine whether a clause or phrase is restrictive or nonrestrictive only by referring to the preceding sentence or sentences.

Prior to moving to Beijing in 1989, Matzger had briefly studied Oriental languages at Berkeley. But when he arrived in China, he discovered that the academic training had not prepared him to understand what he heard in daily conversation. Conversation with natives of Beijing, *which he compared to his experiences in the Berkeley language lab,* quickly taught him that he knew too little Chinese.

[Without the first two sentences, the *which* clause would be restrictive, or necessary to limit the meaning of *conversation.*]

Sometimes, depending on the writer's intended meaning, a clause or phrase may be either restrictive or nonrestrictive. Notice the differences in meaning between the two following sentences, which differ only in punctuation.

Matzger learned that Beijing citizens who spoke a dialect unique to Beijing were especially difficult to understand.

[Without commas around the *who* clause, the sentence suggests that some Beijing citizens speak the Peking dialect and are difficult to understand; other citizens do not speak the dialect and are less difficult to understand.]

Matzger learned that Beijing citizens, who spoke a dialect unique to Beijing, were especially difficult to understand.

[Set off by commas, the *who* clause suggests that all Beijing citizens speak the Peking dialect and are difficult to understand.]

Parenthetical elements, nonrestrictive appositives, absolute and contrasted elements, and words in direct address are set off by commas.

Parenthetical elements include a variety of constructions that introduce supplementary information to a sentence or that make up transitions between sentences.

We read several articles, *such as "Holes in the Great Wall" and "Astigmatism among Pandas,"* about China.

[In this sentence *such as* introduces a nonrestrictive phrase. In the sentence "An essay *such as 'Holes in the Great Wall'* explains that the wall constantly needs repair," *such as* introduces a restrictive phrase. Notice also that when a comma is used with *such as,* the comma comes before *such,* with no comma after *as.*]

"If you visit China," *says Adam Matzger,* "you must visit the wall."

[An expression such as *Adam Matzger says* (*claims, replies,* and so on) is considered parenthetical.

Matzger, *as well as some other recent writers,* is not optimistic about the plight of the panda.

[Expressions like *as well as, in addition to,* and *along with* usually introduce parenthetical matter.]

In fact, Matzger believes that the panda will become extinct in the wild.

[A transitional expression such as *in fact* is always considered parenthetical.]

A Chinese naturalist, who also has been helping Matzger improve his *language skills,* is the source of information about the panda population.

[A subordinate clause may introduce parenthetical matter.]

Appositives are usually set off by commas, though on a few occasions they are restrictive.

The essay *"The Language of Pandas"* combines Matzger's interests in language and in pandas.

[The title of the essay is a restrictive appositive needed to identify which essay is being referred to; thus it is not set off with commas.]

"The Language of Pandas," *a recent article in Smithsonian magazine,* examines the rhetorical importance of pandas in China's foreign relations.

[The appositive is nonrestrictive; thus it is set off with commas.]

Absolute phrases are verbal phrases that are preceded by their subjects. They affect the meaning of the entire sentence in which they appear (not just a single word, phrase, or clause). Absolute phrases are always set off by commas.

According to Matzger, the Chinese authorities are trying to protect panda habitat, *the pandas' needs effectively countering the human desire to create more arable land.*

[The verbal *countering* has its own subject, *needs.*]

Contrasted elements are always set off by comas.

Matzger believes that the survival of the pandas, *not China's concerns for its exploding population,* should decide land use.

Words in direct address do just what you would expect them to do: they address someone or something directly. They are always set off by commas.

"Do not lose this unique symbol of your country, *China,* by bowing to short-term concerns," Matzger seems to be saying.

Geographical names and items in dates and addresses (except zip codes) are set off by commas.

Send your application by April 14, 2005, to Box 289, Murfreesboro, Tennessee 37132.

Dates are sometimes written and punctuated differently in official documents and reports.

On Friday, 21 March 1995, the finalists checked into the hotel.

When only the month and the year are given, no comma is necessary.

By the end of May 2004 the contest will be over.

Unnecessary commas

Superfluous or misplaced commas make sentences difficult to read.

The comma is the most frequently used punctuation mark. It is also the most frequently *mis*used punctuation mark. While trying to master the correct use of the comma, many people tend to overuse it and to misplace it in sentence patterns, especially if they rely too much on the pause test for placement. Some short-winded writers, who pause after every third or fourth word, fill their sentences with commas that make the writing difficult to follow. In the following examples, the large boldface commas should not be included.

Confusing   Students **,** who are interested in Asian literature **,** should take Professor Strawman's seminar **,** in summer term.

Actually, this sentence requires no internal punctuation at all, because the clauses and phrases that have been added to the basic sentence pattern are all restrictive; they are necessary to define or to limit the meaning of the words they modify.

Correct   Students who are interested in Asian literature should take Professor Strawman's seminar in summer term.

Do not use a comma to separate the subject from its verb or the verb from its complement.

Remember that commas are used to set off nonrestrictive or parenthetical additions. Do not use them to separate the parts of the basic (subject-verb-complement) sentence.

Studying Asian literature **,** will occupy my whole summer.

[The subject, *studying,* should not be separated by a comma from its verb *will occupy.*]

Most of my friends agree **,** that we have much to learn from this literature.

[The verb, *agree,* should not be separated by a comma from its complement, the *that* clause.]

Do not use a comma after a coordinating conjunction; do not use a comma before a coordinating conjunction when only a word, phrase, or subordinate clause (rather than a main clause) follows the conjunction.

The first story by Ly Lee tells of his life as a musician, and **,** it contains the songs he used to sing.

[The comma comes **before, not after,** the coordinating conjunction.]

Lee also farmed **,** but never was able to abandon completely his art.

[compound predicate—no comma before *but*]

Do not use commas to set off words or short phrases (especially introductory ones) that are not parenthetical or that are very slightly so.

Before class , we should listen to the audio tape that came with the stories.

The songs , to Lee , represent a link to his country's past.

Do not use commas to set off restrictive clauses, phrases, or appositives.

The book , *Lost in the Highlands* , recounts Lee's many trips to the mountains.

[No commas are needed because the title *Lost in the Highlands* is a restrictive appositive needed to define or limit *book*.]

The end of the book is so moving , that all of us in the class were close to tears.

[No comma is needed because the *that* clause is necessary to define or limit *moving*.]

Readers , trying to understand the writing style , must remember it comes from an oral tradition.

[No commas are needed because the verbal phrase is a restrictive addition needed to define or limit *readers*.]

Do not use a comma before the first or after the last item in a series.

Journals such as , *Asian Literature, Travel,* and *Esquire* , have reviewed his book.

Commas between Main Clauses

Name_____   Score _____

DIRECTIONS In the following sentences, insert an inverted caret (V) wherever two main elements are joined. Then insert either a comma or a semicolon after the first main clause. Write the mark that you added in the blank at the right as well. If a sentence does not have two main clauses, write *C* in the blank to show that the sentence is correct and needs no punctuation mark.

EXAMPLES

My mother grew aloe in an orange pot that was shaped like a fat carrot.   _____*C*_____

We kids often fell and skinned our knees, V and our first choice of treatment was the aloe plant.   _____,_____

1. When we were at the store today, I noticed that many labels advertise "aloe" as an important ingredient.   _____

2. It is especially common in shampoos and liquid soaps often include it.   _____

3. Aloe consists of about 95 percent water so it cannot tolerate freezing temperatures.   _____

4. I remember my mother taking her aloe plants out onto the deck in early spring some of them eventually would flower.   _____

5. The flowers appeared on a stalk in the middle of the plant hummingbirds loved the nectar from those flowers.   _____

6. If we had an accident, Mother cut off a leaf and sliced it open.   _____

7. The leaf is filled with a gelatinous substance that substance contains the healing power of the plant.   _____

8. We put it on burns, skinned places, little cuts, and poison ivy.   _____

9. My grandmother encouraged us to drink a potion she made by mixing the gel with water but we declined her request.   _____

10. I know now that aloe is a common ingredient in herbal medicines and has the reputation of being good for many ailments.   _____

11. Because it is so easy to grow and is an attractive plant, farmers in several states are growing it as a crop.   _____

12. We have visited an aloe farm in California and my sister lives near one in Texas.   _____

13. It looks like a tropical plant so great fields of it do look a little out of place in this country.   _____

_____

14. Originally aloe was an African plant but it has been carried all over
the world.   _____

15. Apparently everyone recognized its healing properties and wanted to
take it with them on their travels.   _____

Commas after Introductory Elements

Name_____ **Score** _____

DIRECTIONS After each introductory element, either write a zero (0) to indicate that no comma is needed or add a comma. Also write the zero or the comma in the blank.

EXAMPLES

Speaking slowly and carefully, my grandmother told her story of moving across the country when she was young. _____,_____

In 1950° she and my grandfather moved from Alabama to California. ____O____

1. When they married my grandmother was only eighteen. _____

2. As a good student she entered college at sixteen. _____

3. While attending college her first semester she went to a party at a friend's house. _____

4. During the next two years she dated the young man she met at the party. _____

5. While he attended the University of Alabama he worked in a plant nursery. _____

6. Because my grandmother also loved plants the two made friends quickly. _____

7. Over the weekends or holidays she helped him with his job. _____

8. Eventually they decided to marry and start their own business. _____

9. In fact Grandmother says they decided to start their own nursery. _____

10. After they learned of a nursery for sale in northern California they decided to try to buy it. _____

11. Without ever actually seeing it they took a big chance. _____

12. Knowing another nursery owner in the same part of the state proved helpful. _____

13. After he learned what they needed he recommended a lawyer who could handle the transaction long distance. _____

14. Usually quiet and conservative they could also be daring and brave. _____

15. Refusing to look back they loaded their few possessions in an old Ford station wagon and drove off to an unknown future. _____

Commas between Items in a Series
and between Coordinate Adjectives

Name_____   **Score** _____

DIRECTIONS In each sentence identify each series that needs commas by writing *1, 2, 3,* and so on above the items and in the blank on the right; identify coordinate adjectives by writing *a, b,* and *c* above the adjectives and in the blank. Insert commas or semicolons where they belong in the sentence and also in the blank to show the punctuation of the pattern. Write *C* in the blank if a sentence has no items in a series or no coordinate adjectives that need punctuation.

EXAMPLES

My grandmother moved her most prized plants to her new home:

1   *2*   *3*   *4*
many herbs, a few azaleas, some daylilies, and some iris.

1,2,3,
and 4

a   b
During the drive she worried about the small sickly basil plants.

_a, b_

1. My very favorite image is of the plants arranged on makeshift shelves in the back of the station wagon.

_____

2. They visited relatives in several cities during the trip, including Dallas Denver and Sacramento.

_____

3. The faded ragged photos of the trip are prized possessions.

_____

4. For her birthday last year we copied the photos had them enlarged and created a montage.

_____

5. In one photo a tall spiky aloe is clearly visible.

_____

6. I have an aloe that looks just like it on a wooden baker's rack in my kitchen.

_____

7. My great-grandmother gave an aloe to my grandmother she gave one of its "pups" to my mother and my mother gave a pup to me.

_____

8. I like knowing that my little aloe plant is a direct living tie to my past.

_____

9. When my children move away from home, I will give them little living reminders of their pasts.

_____

10. Like me, they can use their living reminders to soothe burns heal cuts and quiet crying children.

_____

Commas to Set Off Nonrestrictive Clauses
and Phrases and Parenthetical Elements

Exercise 6-4

Name_____ Score _____

DIRECTIONS In the following sentences, set off each nonrestrictive or parenthetical addition with a comma or commas. Then in the blank write (1) a dash followed by a comma (—,) if the nonrestrictive or parenthetical addition begins the sentence, (2) a comma followed by a dash (,—) if the nonrestrictive or parenthetical addition ends the sentence, (3) a dash enclosed within commas (,—,) if the nonrestrictive or parenthetical addition comes within the sentence, or (4) *C* if there is no nonrestrictive or parenthetical addition to set off.

EXAMPLE

"Starla, you must cut the lawn," my mother said.　　　　_____—,_____

1. Because my family is in the plant business it seems inevitable that I make it my profession.　　　_____

2. Today I remain unsure about my plans.　　　_____

3. I want a job that will not keep me in an office something that lets me set my own hours.　　　_____

4. Last summer I worked for a road contractor a woman my mother has known for years.　　　_____

5. I learned how to operate some big machinery but not however how to survey a work site.　　　_____

6. We worked on the new bypass all summer where it connects with I-40.　　　_____

7. Although I enjoyed the experience I don't want to do that kind of work again.　　　_____

8. The company owner who also was once married to my uncle let me work in a variety of jobs.　　　_____

9. If I learned several jobs I could get a better sense of how suited I am to that kind of work.　　　_____

10. At the summer's end she often said I would know what to do.　　　_____

11. As one would expect many women worked on my construction crew.　　　_____

12. Not surprisingly they worked at every possible task.　　　_____

13. I became friends with one woman who drove a road grader.　　　_____

14. She had worked during the winter clearing roads in the Sierra Nevada a job I would not want.　　　_____

15. The snow often completely closes roads there, and she drove a machine that plowed the snow off the roads.   _____

16. "I drove on roads I could not even see" she said "but I never had an accident."   _____

17. Although she was very small and was dwarfed by the machinery I learned to have complete confidence in her.   _____

18. She could do delicate work with the big machines work that some drivers could not match.   _____

19. Her name was Sierra a name she gave herself in memory of her love of the mountains.   _____

20. When I left that job at the end of the summer she gave me an aloe plant.   _____

All Uses of the Comma

Name _____ **Score** _____

DIRECTIONS Decide whether each comma used in the following sentences (a) separates main clauses, (b) sets off an introductory addition, (c) separates items is a series or coordinate adjectives, or (d) sets off a parenthetical or nonrestrictive addition. Write *a, b, c,* or *d* above each comma and in the blank to the right of the sentence.

EXAMPLE

    d   *d*
Let us consider, for a moment, the virtues of the aloe plant.   _____*d*_____

1. My mother has always grown herbs, dried them, and fashioned them into wreathes. _____

2. She decorated our house with them, gave them as gifts, and occasionally sold a few. _____

3. Now she has started her own company, an Internet company. _____

4. When she began surfing the Internet, she saw an opportunity to sell more of her herbs. _____

5. "Rachel," she asked me, "will you teach me how to make Web pages?" _____

6. I taught her basic HTML and showed her useful Web sites, especially htmlgoodies.com. _____

7. Before long she was getting orders for herbal wreaths, and she worked steadily at filling them. _____

8. Her sister Ruth, who recently was a guest on *Jeopardy,* offered to help make the wreaths. _____

9. When I came home from school, Mother had moved everything out of the garage and converted it into a work space. _____

10. My fun-loving, industrious mother had become an entrepreneur. _____

11. Now two workers are responsible just for shipping, several more create wreaths, and nine others work at her nursery. _____

12. I can't keep up with the changes, but I think she now also sells dried herbs. _____

13. "If I don't grow my business," she says, "it will die." _____

14. She tends it like her garden, like it is a growing thing in need of her care. _____

15. Although I have seen her more relaxed, I have never seen her happier. _____

All Uses of the Comma

Name_____   Score _____

DIRECTIONS In the following sentences, insert all necessary commas. Then write *a, b, c,* or *d* in the blank to the right of each sentence to indicate that the comma (a) separates main clauses, (b) sets off an introductory addition, (c) separates items in a series or coordinate adjectives, or (d) sets off a parenthetical or nonrestrictive addition.

EXAMPLE

When Mother began her Internet company, our lives were changed.   *b*

1. It started as a small business but it soon grew into a sizable enterprise.   _____

2. With her lively sense of humor she helps us keep a healthy perspective on this new challenge in our lives.   _____

3. The new nursery is near Sacramento California.   _____

4. She grows herbs succulents and perennials there.   _____

5. The nursery has grown into a large business but she sells only herbal wreathes and dried herbs through her Internet site.   _____

6. She has been talking to her lawyer lately preparing to expand the business again.   _____

7. Her passion for business fueled by this early success is growing.   _____

8. When I am home from school I help her.   _____

9. She often asks me to work on the Web site to help with filling orders or to repair machinery at the nursery.   _____

10. I am her one indispensable worker and she laughs because I can do so many different jobs.   _____

11. Local newspapers have run several stories on this new successful company.   _____

12. Readers are fascinated by my mother's daring by her success and by her optimism.   _____

13. She thinks she has succeeded because she has insisted on having fun at her job and I agree with her.   _____

14. After I have watched her succeed I know I will never take a job that does not give me the same joy.   _____

All Uses of the Comma

Name_____   **Score** _____

DIRECTIONS Write a sentence to illustrate each of the items listed.

EXAMPLE

an absolute element

According to my Mother we need to vote next week, our vote potentially helping Alice to win a close race.

1. a complete date

2. a nonrestrictive clause

3. a contrasted element

4. a restrictive phrase

5. a transitional expression

6. items in a series

7. a parenthetical element introduced by *such as*

8. two main clauses linked by a coordinating conjunction

9. an introductory verbal phrase

10. a complete address, including zip code

Superfluous Commas

Name_____   **Score** _____

DIRECTIONS Each of the following sentences is correctly punctuated. Explain why a comma is not added to each sentence at the place or places indicated in the question.

EXAMPLE

I knew my mother would succeed when she started
her new business.
Why is there no comma before *when?*   *adverb clause at*
                                                    end of the sentence

1. A botanist like Professor Lavery can change the way we
   look at wildflowers.
   Why is *like Professor Lavery* not set off by commas?   _____

2. Like Professor Dunne he inspired me to photograph
   wildflowers.
   Why is there no comma after *Dunne?*   _____

3. He was the teacher in my first photography class
   and introduced me to nature photography.
   Why is there not a comma before *and?*   _____

4. I wanted to take a trip to the Ansel Adams Gallery this
   summer, but I could not afford the trip.
   Why is there no comma after *but?*   _____

5. Until this year my favorite locations for nature
   photography had been in the Smokey Mountains
   National Park.
   Why is *for nature photography* not set off by commas?   _____

6. I have learned that I work best in early morning light.
   Why is there no comma after *learned?*   _____

7. My big telephoto lenses get heavy after a long day of
   hiking.
   Why is there no comma after *big?*   _____

8. The work produced after I am tired is often not very good.
   Why is *after I am tired* not set off by commas?   _____

9. The term "tired" has several definitions.
   Why is *tired* not set off by commas?   _____

10. The definition that fits this context is "physically
    and mentally exhausted."
    Why is *that fits this context* not set off by commas?   _____

11. I cannot take good photographs unless I am rested,
    but I can scout for good locations for the next morning.
    Why is there no comma after *but?*   _____

12. My photograph *Bugling Elk* is my most famous work.
    Why is *Bugling Elk* not set off by commas?   _____

13. Ironically, I took that photograph of a bugling elk on
    a golf course in Estes Park, Colorado.
    Why is *of a bugling elk* not set off by commas?   _____

14. He was part of a herd that wintered on the golf course,
    but his life ended prematurely.
    Why is there no comma after *but?*   _____

15. Samson the bugling elk is memorialized by a statue
    in Estes Park.
    Why is there no comma after *Samson?*   _____

Use the semicolon between parts of equal grammatical rank: (a) between two main clauses not joined by a coordinating conjunction and (b) between coordinate elements that already contain commas. The semicolon indicates that one part of a coordinate construction is finished.

> We divided the class into three groups, each with six students; each of the groups is studying an impressionist painter.

[two main clauses with no coordinating conjunction]

> Alice's group is studying Mary Cassatt, particularly three paintings in outdoor settings: *Woman Reading in a Garden; Woman Holding a Red Zinnia;* and *Lydia Crocheting in the Garden at Marly,* a portrait of Cassatt's sister.

[items in a series, some of which contain commas]

Connecting independent clauses

Use the semicolon to connect two main clauses not joined by a coordinating conjunction or two main clauses that contain commas and are also joined by a coordinating conjunction.

PATTERN   MAIN CLAUSE; MAIN CLAUSE

> I wanted to read an interview of Cassatt; Alice could not find an interview of her in the library.

[two main clauses with no coordinating conjunction]

> The librarian helped us find Cassatt's correspondence with Degas, Monet, and Manet; so we used those in our report.

[The first clause already contains commas, so a semicolon must be used before the coordinating conjunction *so.*]

Caution: In a divided quotation, be especially careful to use a semicolon between the two main clauses of a sentence when they are not connected by a coordinating conjunction.

"We need slides of the paintings," Alice said; "we need to think about a mixed media presentation."

Remember that a conjunctive adverb, like *however,* or a transitional expression, like *for example,* is not the same as a coordinating conjunction—*and, but, or, nor, for, so,* and *yet.* Thus when a conjunctive adverb or a transitional expression is used to link two main clauses, a semicolon must come before it.

Alice wrote the text for our presentation; *however,* I made all of the slides.

Separating elements that contain commas

Use the semicolon to separate a series of equal elements which themselves contain commas.

We concluded our presentation with a series of questions: what themes do you find in Cassatt's paintings; what can you say now about her frequent use of children as subjects; with our next presentation in mind, which paintings would you like us to explore in more depth?

I knew that the group would work well together—that Alice would be a quiet, determined leader; that Jennifer would be eager and bright; and that Andy would seem too quiet, but would surprise with his insights.

Semicolons

Name _____ **Score** _____

DIRECTIONS In the following sentences insert an inverted caret (∨) between main clauses and add semicolons as needed. In the blank, copy the semicolon and the word or transitional expression immediately following, along with the comma if there is one. Write *C* in the blank if the sentence is correctly punctuated. (Not all sentences have two main clauses.)

EXAMPLE

Cryseyde has a print of a Mary Cassatt painting in her office;∨ quite fittingly it hangs near a drawing of the Wife of Bath, Chaucer's most famous female character.

; quite fittingly

1. We saw the painting first at the Chicago Art Institute it is one of the institute's best paintings.

_____

2. The child sits in the mother's lap its feet are in a basin.

_____

3. Her left arm curls around the child's waist her right hand holds the child's foot.

_____

4. The mother's hands are in sharp focus however, much of the rest is rendered in soft brush strokes.

_____

5. Having the hands in sharp focus draws the viewer's attention the viewer must contemplate the significance of the hands.

_____

6. A woman's hands often symbolize her nurturing ability, her creative ability, and her ability to lead a child to knowledge they embody Cassatt's favorite themes.

_____

7. There is nothing sentimental about the painting it is quite realistic.

_____

8. The mother's hands seem slightly red and raw in fact, she seems caught in a quiet moment in an otherwise busy day.

_____

9. She was clearly sympathetic to her models however, she avoided sentimental portraits

_____

10. Both mother and child appear quiet and gentle their bodies are relaxed and open.

_____

11. When Cassatt was very young, her parents began taking her on trips to Europe she was born in Pittsburgh but grew up in Philadelphia.

_____

12. By the time she was ten she had seen most of the major cities of Europe as her parents had planned, she learned much from travel.

_____

13. Cassatt chose career over marriage she returned to Europe
    at the age of twenty-one to study art.   _____

14. This must have been a hard decision for her parents to
    accept although they had raised her to be independent,
    they probably never expected this much independence.   _____

15. Cassatt became the first internationally important American
    woman painter fortunately, her parents lived to enjoy
    her success with her.   _____

Commas and Semicolons

Exercise 7-2

Name_____ Score _____

DIRECTIONS In the following sentences insert either a semicolon or a comma as needed and also in the blank.

EXAMPLE

"You need to come with me to Boston," Alice said; "we can see the Cassatt exhibition."

;_____

1. She was the only American to exhibit with the Impressionists and was friends with Renoir Manet, and Degas.

_____

2. She traveled alone, had a good head for business and refused to let anyone dictate how she should paint.

_____

3. Like other Impressionists she was influenced by the old masters but she already was developing her own style.

_____

4. During her travels across Europe she often copied paintings that she admired and she learned technique from them.

_____

5. Before settling in Paris in 1874 she lived and studied in Rome, Parma and Seville.

_____

6. Her paintings of this period reveal the influence of old masters combined with her interest in modern subjects: a woman, perhaps her sister, flirting; a young woman offering a drink to a bullfighter a woman tossing flowers.

_____

7. "She was fearless," said Degas "and determined to define herself on her own terms."

_____

8. She learned much from Degas in fact, seeing one of his paintings of ballerinas was the turning point in her life as an artist.

_____

9. After she saw it she said she began "to live."

_____

10. Although Degas was a notoriously difficult man he and Cassatt became good friends.

_____

11. He asked her to join the Impressionists a group of like-minded painters who showed their art together.

_____

12. For the next twenty-five years she created a remarkable body of work in pastels, drawings and paintings.

_____

13. She depicted modern women going to the opera, reading and caring for children.

_____

14. The model was often a member of her family—for example her
    sister.   _____

15. She often painted a woman holding a child up to pick fruit a
    fitting symbol for Cassatt who generously passed her knowledge
    to us all.   _____

UNIT 8

Apostrophe

Hodges': chapter 15
Writer's: chapter 33

Use the apostrophe (a) to indicate the possessive case—except for personal pronouns, (b) to mark omissions in contracted words and numerals, and (c) to form certain plurals.
  The apostrophe, in most of its uses, indicates that something has been omitted.

don't   [do not]

they're   [they *are*]

children's books   [books *of* or *for* children]

the artist's paintings   [paintings *of* or *by* the artist]

Showing possession

In general, a noun or a pronoun does not come immediately before another noun or pronoun: we do not write "children books" or "artist painting." When we do need to use a noun or pronoun before another noun or pronoun, we make the first one possessive by using an apostrophe. In a sense, we say that the first noun or pronoun owns the second one.

parent's duty   [duty of one parent]

parents' duty   [duty of two or more parents]

everyone's duty   [duty of everyone]

crater's edge   [edge of the crater]

craters' edges   [edges of the craters]

Add the apostrophe and an *s* (*'s*) to a noun or indefinite pronoun to indicate the singular possessive case.

The poet's picture hung on the president's wall.

One's questions often go unanswered.

Option: To form the possessive case of a singular noun that ends in *s*, add either the apostrophe and s or only the apostrophe.

James' essay   OR   James's essay

Columbus' ship   OR   Columbus's ship

Add the apostrophe (') to all plural nouns that end in *s* to indicate the plural possessive case. Add the apostrophe and an *s* (*'s*) to all plural nouns not ending in *s* to indicate the plural possessive case.

Always form the plural of the noun first. Then, if the plural noun ends in *s*, add only the apostrophe to show the possessive case.

photographer [singular]   photographers [plural]

dignitary [singular]   dignitaries [plural]

The photographer's pictures hung in several dignitaries' offices.

If the plural noun does not end in *s*, add the apostrophe and an *s* to show the possessive case.

man [singular]   men [plural]

woman [singular]   women [plural]

Men's and women's photographs are exhibited in the Ansel Adams Gallery.

Add the apostrophe and an *s* to the last word of compounds or word groups.

my father-in-law's car

someone else's turn

the secretary of state's position

Add the apostrophe and an *s* to each name to indicate individual ownership, but to only the final name to indicate joint ownership.

Josh's and Sarah's work crews are cleaning Mill Creek.

[Josh and Sarah have different work crews.]

Josh and Sarah's work crew is cleaning Mill Creek.

[Josh and Sarah have one work crew.]

To indicate a relationship comparable to ownership, add the apostrophe, especially in time relationships, in academic titles, and before gerunds.

Josh's having to photograph the clean-up led to the local television stations' broadcasting his photographs of the event.

[*Josh's* is possessive because of the gerund *having*. And *station's* is possessive because of the gerund *broadcasting*.]

He argued that he had earned a master's degree in photography in an hour's time.

With contractions and numbers

Be careful to place the apostrophe exactly where the omission occurs.

The class of '00 [2000] can't [cannot] decide what to include in the time capsule that's [that is] to be buried on the town square.

Forming certain plurals

Use the apostrophe and an *s* to form the plural of lowercase letters. If needed to prevent confusion, the apostrophe and an *s* can be used to form the plural of figures, symbols, abbreviations, and words referred to as words, but frequently only an *s* is added.

final *k's*

the 1970's   OR   the 1970s

V.F.W.'s   OR   V.F.W.s

and's   OR   ands

Unnecessary apostrophes

The apostrophe is not needed for possessive pronouns—*his, hers, its, ours, yours, theirs,* and *whose*—or for plural pronouns not in the possessive case.

Whose photographs are these—*yours* or *theirs?*

Her company regularly takes senior photographs at the *Joneses.*

[*Joneses* is plural but not possessive.]

Apostrophe

Name_____ **Score** _____

DIRECTIONS Add all apostrophes needed in the following sentences. In the blank enter each word, number, or letter to which you have added an apostrophe. Be careful not to add needless apostrophes. If a sentence is correct, write *C* in the blank.

EXAMPLE

There's no apostrophe after the *s* in the word group "ethics rules."   *There's*

1. Josh Allen, Jr.s autobiography portrays an extraordinary life.   _____

2. Local residents know little about him aside from the facts recorded on a plaque near the town square.   _____

3. The facts of Allens life are indisputable since he carefully recorded them before his death in 1939.   _____

4. His autobiography languished in the local library until a student unearthed it while doing research for a paper on Veterans Day.   _____

5. The student found a reference to Allen in Joshua Wilcoxs memoir about serving in World War II.   _____

6. Prior to entering the Navy in 1941, Wilcox had lived here with his best friends parents.   _____

7. He knew of Allens autobiography and read it in the library.   _____

8. He even tried to convince a local publisher to publish it as a tribute to all veterans.   _____

9. Allen served for two years in the first world war and his accounts of his experiences in battle are riveting.   _____

10. He even includes stories of having met Wilfred Owen, a British soldier who became the wars chronicler.   _____

11. Allen is at his best when his writing plumbs a soldiers average day.   _____

12. Allen knew instinctively that his readers interests lay in the behavior of ordinary men in extraordinary circumstances.   _____

13. His description of life in the trenches has been cited by later authors as the definitive treatment of the subject.   _____

14. One suspects, after reading Allen, that the soldiers mental toughness must have been strained as much as their physical abilities.   _____

15. He is particularly good at creating images of the wet, cold, filthy conditions that were a soldiers daily lot.   _____

16. We discussed the memoir in class and agreed that none of us had appreciated the sacrifices made by the soldiers.   _____

17. We have decided to devote one of our papers to other authors who have written about the wars effects on soldiers.   _____

18. We will read Robert Graves autobiography *Goodbye to All That*.   _____

19. And we will read all of Wilfred Owens poetry.   _____

20. We certainly understand now why the town erected the plaque to commemorate Allens sacrifice.   _____

Apostrophe

Name_____ **Score** _____

DIRECTIONS Rewrite the following word groups as a noun or a pronoun preceded by another noun or pronoun in the possessive case.

EXAMPLES

a responsibility of everybody

everybody's responsibility

the responsibilities of the United Nations

the United Nations' responsibility

1. the records of NOW

2. a poem by Sharon Olds

3. the opinions of the investigators

4. the representative of the United States

5. the skeletons of the dinosaurs

6. an invitation sent by Mr. and Mrs. Jones

7. the antennae of the moth

8. an address by the governor of Massachusetts

9. the interests of the babies

10. a telescope shared by Tim and Tracey

11. the example of the women

12. a reunion at the Burtons

13. opinions held by one

14. the angle of the eclipse

15. the apprentices to Hephaestus

16. the riddle of the Sphinx

17. the visits of Anna and Adam to the Caymus vineyard

18. the lawnmower of the son-in-law

19. the hood of the Toyota

20. the word processor of Jennifer

UNIT 9 Quotation Marks

Hodges': chapter 16
Writer's: chapter 34

Direct quotations and dialogue

When you use quotation marks, you let your reader know that you are quoting directly (that is, you are stating in the exact words) what someone has written, said, or thought.

"Will you return this book to the library for me?" Victoria asked.

"I'll be glad to," I told her. But I thought to myself, "I think I will check it out in my name and read it this weekend."

Use quotation marks for direct quotations and in all dialogue. Set off long quotations by indention.
Use double quotation marks (" ") before and after all direct quotations.

Direct Quotation	She asked me, "Do you want to visit Nashville?"
Direct Quotation	The tour guide booklet recommends a visit to the *Grand Old Opry*, "the longest running radio broadcast in America."
	[A phrase from the booklet is quoted.]

Do not use quotation marks with indirect quotations.

Indirect Quotation	She asked me if I wanted to visit Nashville.
Indirect Quotation	I told her that we could drive there this afternoon.
	[*That* frequently introduces an indirect quotation.]

Use a single quotation mark (' ') before and after a quotation within a quotation.

Quotation within a Quotation	David asked, "Did you see the exhibit 'Mississippi Plains Indians' in the Cumberland Museum?"

In quoting dialogue (conversation), a new paragraph begins each time the speaker changes.

Eleven-year-old John proudly announced to his brother, "I scored 9700 points today on the new computer game."

"That's great. You even beat Jeff's best score," replied nine-year-old Andrew.

"When we get home from school today, I'll show you how to play," promised John.

"Okay, but I will have to do my homework first," said Andrew, "and then you can show me."

Note: Commas set off expressions such as *he said* that introduce, interrupt, or follow direct quotations.

Their mother reminded, "Boys, be sure to turn off the computer before you go to bed."

"Boys," their mother reminded, "be sure to turn off the computer before you go to bed."

"Boys, be sure to turn off the computer before you go to bed," reminded their mother.

If the quoted speech is a question or an exclamation, a question mark or exclamation point—instead of a comma—follows the quoted passage.

"John, do not lay that magnet on the computer!" cautioned Marilyn. "It could ruin your hard disk."

Caution: Remember that a divided quotation made up of two main clauses or two complete sentences must be punctuated with a semicolon or an end mark.

"A magnet can ruin a hard drive or floppy disk," Andrew added; "it also can affect the monitor."

OR

"A magnet can ruin a hard drive or floppy disk," Andrew added. "It can also affect the monitor."

Double quotation marks set off thoughts, as if they were stated.

"Now I know how I lost the file on my floppy disk," thought Boone.

Indent long quotations. When you quote one paragraph or less of prose, all lines of a long quotation (more than four lines if you are using Modern Language Association style, more than forty words if you are using the American Psychological Association style) are indented ten spaces from the left margin and are double-spaced. When you quote two or more paragraphs, indent the first line of each complete paragraph an additional three spaces or an additional five spaces rather than the usual ten. Use quotation marks only if they appear in the original. (If the quotation is run in with the text, remember that it should begin and end with a double quotation mark.)

In *The Creators* Daniel Boorstin devotes chapters to important individuals in the creative history of western civilization. He begins his discussion of Charles Dickens by alluding to G. K. Chesterton's estimate of Dickens.

Even if Dickens had not been a great event in English literature, he would be a great event in English history. For, as G. K. Chesterton reminds us, "the man led a mob. He

did what no English statesman, perhaps, has really done; he called out the people."
Dickens' career was a grand literary love affair with the English public, not just the
reading public but the whole listening public. (364)

Fewer than four lines of poetry may be run into the text. If run in, the quoted material should begin and end with a double quotation mark. Use quotation marks only if they
appear in the original.

The classical poet Sappho often wrote brief poems whose effect depended on
metaphorical contrast. In this poem she presents love in terms of a serpent's venom
which she describes as "Irresistible/and bittersweet/that loosener/of limbs."

[Use a slash to mark the end of a line when poetry is run into the text.]

OR

The classical poet Sappho was particularly skilled at extending a metaphor as the
central structure for an entire poem. Here she compares love to a serpent's venom:

With his venom
Irresistible
and bittersweet
that loosener
of limbs, Love
reptile-like
strikes me down.

Titles of short works

Use quotation marks for minor titles—of short works such as television shows, short
stories, essays, short poems, one-act plays, songs, articles from periodicals—and for sub-
divisions of books.

For her senior thesis Victoria examined the poems in Sharon Olds's collection *The
Dead and the Living,* and concentrated on "New Mother" and "Ecstasy."

Beth Nielsen Chapman writes and sings beautiful songs about sometimes surprising
subjects. In "Child Again" she sings of an elderly woman in a nursing home, in "Emily"
she sings of visiting a sick friend, and somehow both songs are hauntingly beautiful.

Words used in a special sense

In this example the context requires that the words be emphasized with quotation marks.

The term "research paper" is broadly applied to anything from a three-source,
five-page paper to a one-hundred-source, book-length doctoral dissertation.

[*Research paper* may be either italicized or enclosed in quotation marks.]

However, avoid the tendency some writers have of using quotation marks freely through-
out a paper to call attention to what they consider clever phrasings. Often what they think

are clever phrases are really only trite expressions, slang, or colloquialisms that could be better phrased, and quotation marks will not elevate the writing.

Ineffective	The computer was "up to" more of its "strange" ways: it "wasted" crew members one by one.
Better	The computer demonstrated a terrifying intelligence: it killed the crew methodically and mercilessly.

Quotation marks should not enclose titles that head compositions. Quotation marks also should not enclose a cliché or mark a *yes* or *no* in indirect discourse.

Yes, he did accuse her of beating around the bush.

NOT

"Yes," he did accuse her of "beating around the bush."

Placement of other punctuation with quotation marks

Follow the conventions of American printers in deciding whether various marks of punctuation belong inside or outside the quotation marks.

The period and the comma are usually placed inside the quotation marks.

"Well," he said, "I am ready to hear Mike Dash read from his new book."

Exception: If you are citing a page reference for a quotation, place the comma or the period after the page citation—and thus after the quotation marks.

Dash's *Tulip Mania* begins, "They came from all over Holland, dressed like crows in black from head to foot and journeying along frozen tracks rendered treacherous by the scars of a thousand hooves and narrow wheels" (1).

The semicolon and the colon are placed outside the quotation marks.

He read the instructions on the VHS cassette labeled "Jill Hague": "Return by Wednesday, 3:00 P.M."

Another cassette was labeled "William Connelly"; it contained a tape of his recent lecture on the Wife of Bath.

The dash, the question mark, and the exclamation point are placed inside the quotation marks when they apply to the quoted matter and outside the quotation marks when they apply to the whole sentence.

"Where is my saddle?" asked Jennifer.

[The question mark applies to the quoted material.]

Did you notice the bill marked "Pay today"?

[The question mark applies to the whole sentence.]

At what point did he say, "Why are you telling me this?"

[a question within a question—one question mark inside the quotation marks]

Quotation Marks

Name_____ **Score** _____

DIRECTIONS In the sentences below, insert all needed quotation marks. Then enter the quotation marks and the first and last word of each quoted part in the blanks. Be sure to include the other marks of punctuation used with the quotation marks in their proper position—either inside or outside the quotation marks. Do not enclose an indirect quotation. Write *C* in the blank if a sentence is correct without quotation marks.

EXAMPLE

My father-in-law always said, "That was mighty good, Mrs. Pearson," as he rose to leave the table after the noon meal.

"That . . . Pearson,"

1. For a story in her creative writing class, Helene tried to capture the dialect and regional language that she had heard as a child. For example, one of her characters sprayed two fighting dogs with a hose-pipe, a term used for garden hose.

_____

2. The main character is an old woman who greets her husband after a long day with the question, Well, have you eat yet?

_____

3. There is much talk of food. Mrs. Poulin refers to a mixture of turnip greens, collards, and mustard greens, as simply greens.

_____

4. Be sure to put some fatback in the greens, Mr. Poulin reminds her. They won't taste right without the fatback.

_____

5. Although Mr. Poulin seems perfectly healthy, Mrs. Poulin seems convinced his end is imminent. She often prefaces her sentences with the remark, When something happens to John . . . .

_____

6. Now Lavinia, he will say, nothing is going to happen to me anytime soon.

_____

7. Mr. Poulin is also fond of naming machinery that he uses. The most memorable names include Fred for his tiller, Roy for his car, and Theodore for his bandsaw.

_____

8. This tendency toward the bizarre in naming applies to the names for their children. The daughter is Lourlene Lavinia, referred to by the term Precious; the son is George Washington Poulin, referred to as Big Man.

_____

9. Mrs. Poulin loves to meet acquaintances in Publix and hold up the checkout line while she recounts the latest exploits of Precious and Big Man. You know I don't like to brag, she'll say, but have I told you about Precious's latest accomplishment?

_____

10. The Poulins are composites of many people that I knew growing up, Helene has told me.

_____

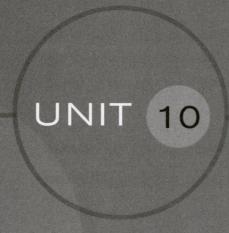

UNIT 10

Other Marks of Punctuation

Hodges': chapter 17
Writer's: chapter 35

The end marks of punctuation give most writers little difficulty except when they are used with direct quotations.

Period

The period follows declarative and mildly imperative (command) sentences, indirect questions, and many abbreviations.

Declarative Sentence	Jayme Cleaveland, director of the Lubbock Writers Project, explains that this semester her students will focus on weather.
Mildly Imperative Sentence	Read about Cleaveland's plans for the workshop next week.
Indirect Question	She was asked if Bill Hall will attend.
Abbreviation	Dr. Lavery also will read from his essay on Hurricane Camille.

Question mark

The question mark follows direct (but not indirect) questions.

Direct Question	Would you like to attend the workshop**?**
Quoted Question	"Will there be an autograph session after David Lavery speaks**?**" I wondered.
	[No comma or period follows the question mark used at the end of a quoted passage.]

Sometimes a declarative or imperative sentence can be made into a question by simply changing the period to a question mark.

The Meteorology Club helped plan the workshop**?**

[Compare "Did the Meteorology Club help plan the workshop?" in which the verb must change to form a question.]

Exclamation point

The exclamation point follows emphatic interjections and statements of strong emotion.

Marla Cartwright's first book examines the formation of tornadoes. "Amazing! Incredible!" cried the audience as they watched her video of the Wichita tornado.

[No comma or period follows the exclamation point used at the end of a quoted passage.]

Avoid using an exclamation point just to make your writing sound exciting or important.

I witnessed the tornado hitting my neighborhood, and I will never forget it.

[The content of the sentence, not an exclamation point at the end, communicates the writer's belief in the importance of the facts.]

Of the internal marks of punctuation (those that do not mark the end of a sentence), the semicolon, the colon, and the dash are most closely related to the period because they bring the reader to a full stop—rather than to a pause as the comma does. Notice the difference between the way you read aloud a sentence that has a comma and one that has a colon, a dash, or a semicolon.

The first speaker was introduced by Sarah Lavery, an award-winning Web master.

[a slight pause for the comma]

The Web Guild named three recipients of the award: Francis Nelson, John Wyatt, and Kozo White.

[a full stop for the colon]

The award carries a large stipend—considerably more than their annual salaries; therefore, they can devote full time to their creative work.

[a full stop for the dash and for the semicolon]

You have already studied the comma, the semicolon, the apostrophe, and quotation marks. As you learn about the other commonly used marks of internal punctuation, you will become aware of the overlapping functions of some punctuation marks—that is, of the occasions when several different marks of punctuation are appropriate.

Colon

The colon, following a main clause, formally introduces a word, a phrase, a clause, or a list. It is also used to separate figures in scriptural and time references and to introduce some quoted sentences.

Following a main clause or sentence pattern, the colon and the dash often may be used interchangeably. The colon is a more formal mark of punctuation than the dash.

For one very good reason the films will be previewed in March: it is National Women's History month.

[The dash is not generally used when a main clause is being introduced.]

Tonight's films will feature three actors: Clint Eastwood, Daffy Duck, and Gene Hackman.

[A dash could also be used to introduce this list.]

Rachel thought of perfect lighting for the aisle: candles in paper bags lining both sides.

All across campus posters advertise the films: "Film Previews Tonight—Follow the Lights."

[The dash is not used to introduce quotations, but it perfectly complements the message of the poster.]

Except for this last example, in which a quotation is introduced following an expression such as *he said* (in this case, *posters advertise*), there is no reason to interrupt a sentence with a colon. Do not use a colon between a subject and verb or between a verb and its complement or object.

Tonight's reviewers will introduce the films, will teach our students how to respond to a film, and will also inspire some of them to want some day to make films.

[A colon after *films* would interrupt the sentence pattern.]

Tonight's program has at least three goals: it will introduce several local film makers; it will teach our students how to respond to films; and it will inspire our students to want some day to make their own films.

[The colon introduces a list of main clauses following a main sentence pattern.]

The colon is also used between chapter and verse in scriptural passages and between hours and minutes in time references.

John 3:16

2:15 P.M.

Dash

Like the colon, the dash may introduce a word, a phrase, a clause, or a list that follows a sentence pattern; unlike the colon, it may interrupt a sentence pattern to mark a sudden break in thought, to set off a parenthetical element for emphasis or clarity, or to set off an introductory list.

When I perform, I am not nervous—unless someone gets up and leaves noisily just as I begin—then I become a nervous wreck.

[Dashes, or sometimes parentheses, are used to set off a sudden break in thought.]

The three judges—McDaniel, Hague, and Connelly—will be in the first row.

[Colons are not used here because they would interrupt the sentence pattern. Commas are not used because the list itself contains commas. Parentheses could be used.]

McDaniel, Hague, and Connelly—they are the three judges, and they will be sitting in the front row.

[The colon is not used here because it would interrupt the sentence pattern. Use the dash when an introductory list precedes the sentence pattern.]

Look into the tent, in the front row, and you will see the three judges—McDaniel, Hague, and Connelly.

[The colon is also appropriate here to set off a list following the sentence pattern.]

Parentheses

Parentheses (1) set off supplementary or illustrative matter, (2) sometimes set off parenthetical matter, and (3) enclose figures or letters used for numbering, as in this sentence.

The primary use of the parentheses is to set off supplementary or illustrative material that is loosely joined to the sentence.

Claustrophobia (the fear of confined spaces) affected a woman in the theater today.

[The parentheses set off the definition; commas could also be used.]

More women than men admit to having xanthelasma (see definition on preceding page).

[A lowercase letter begins the information in parentheses when the material in parentheses forms a part of the sentence.]

Three marks of punctuation are used to set off parenthetical matter. The most commonly used are commas, which cause the reader only to pause and so keep the parenthetical matter closely related to the sentence. The least frequently used are parentheses, which minimize the importance of the parenthetical matter by setting it off distinctly from the sentence. Dashes, the third mark used to enclose parenthetical matter, emphasize the parenthetical matter, since they cause the reader to stop at the beginning and the end of the matter. (Remember that dashes, or sometimes parentheses, are necessary not only for emphasis but for clarity when the parenthetical matter itself includes commas.)

Women are more willing than men, as studies have shown, to admit their fears.

[Commas would be used by most writers to set off this parenthetical matter.]

Women are more willing than men (as studies have shown) to admit their fears.

[Parentheses minimize the importance of the parenthetical matter.]

Women are more willing than men—as studies have shown—to admit their fears.

[Dashes emphasize the parenthetical matter.]

Many factors—such as the size of the audience, the importance of the conference, the quality of her introduction—affect Diana when she performs.

[Dashes are needed for clarity to enclose the parenthetical matter that contains commas. Parentheses could also be used, but they would minimize the importance of the list of factors.]

Brackets

When you need to explain something about a quotation, enclose your explanation within brackets to show that it is not part of the quoted matter.

In Jill McCorkle's story "Migration of the Love Bugs," the narrator says, "My husband and I live in a tin can **[a mobile home]**. He calls it the streamline model, the top of the line, the cream of the crop when it comes to moveable homes."

[The writer of the sentence added *a mobile home* to explain *tin can.*]

Slash

The slash indicates options and shows the end of a line of poetry run in with the text.

In "Still Life with Movement" Gay Brewer first creates the still life: "A pear representing innocence, **/** lies beside a peach, sensuality. **/** The pieces are equally voluptuous." He introduces movement when "all analysis **/** is interrupted by a child's hand" that reaches for the tempting fruit.

[Notice the space before and after each slash in the poetry.]

Ellipses

Use ellipsis points (three spaced periods) to mark an omission from a quoted passage and to mark a reflective pause or hesitation.

The old man looked away, rocking gently, resting his head against the ladderback chair. "Well, maybe I have . . . maybe I haven't," he said. "I disremember."

—Robert Herring

Jill McCorkle's story "Comparison Shopping," like many of her stories, is filled with pop culture references. For example, the narrator says to a prospective boyfriend, "You ought to be on 'Jeopardy' . . . You know more than God."

If ellipsis points are used to indicate that the end of a quoted sentence is being omitted, and if the part that is quoted forms a complete sentence itself, use the sentence period plus ellipsis points.

Equally good are Sherman's chapters on reviewers and journalists. . . .

—*The New York Review of Books*

End Marks of Punctuation

Name_____ **Score** _____

DIRECTIONS Write a sentence to illustrate each of the following uses of an end mark of punctuation.

EXAMPLE

a quoted direct question

Fred asked me, "What dry fly will you use today on the McCloud River?"

1. a mildly imperative sentence

2. a direct question

3. a sentence containing an abbreviation

4. an exclamation

5. a declarative sentence

6. an indirect quotation

7. a declarative sentence containing a quoted direct question

8. an indirect question

9. a declarative sentence containing a quoted exclamation

10. a quotation that includes the ellipsis mark

Internal Marks of Punctuation

Name_____   **Score** _____

DIRECTIONS In the sentences below insert commas, semicolons, dashes, parentheses, and brackets, as needed. Then enter in the blanks the mark or marks you have added. If more than one punctuation mark is possible, choose the one you think most writers would use, but be prepared to discuss the effect of the other possible choice or choices.

EXAMPLE

Mary Oliver's poems, her readers usually realize, are challenging.   , , _____

1. Although they are challenging they also are understandable.   _____

2. She seems intent on generating wonder and enjoyment in her readers she is not interested in perplexing them.   _____

3. The first two lines of "Spring Azures" invoke a lovely scene "In spring the blue azures bow down / at the edges of shallow puddles / to drink the black rain water."   _____

4. Her poems are filed with animals owls deer her beloved dogs.   _____

5. The blue azures bright blue butterflies tempt Oliver to follow them.   _____

6. One critic also believes that "they the butterflies tempt the reader to follow Oliver as she traverses the landscape in words."   _____

7. The blue azure, a butterfly common in open fields is the perfect symbol for Oliver.   _____

8. Oliver's poems always are about seeing, so the word common invites us to see the extraordinary beauty this ordinary creature brings to our lives.   _____

9. The poem begins the journey, it introduces our guide and it sets the tone of the journey.   _____

10. We are all on the same journey Oliver suggests.   _____

11. In another poem Oliver refers to an owl as an "angel" and as a "buddha with wings" striking images linked to its role as the agent of death.   _____

12. She examines the snow in the morning for signs of the owl a bloody patch where it has found its prey.   _____

13. Marking this patch of snow are other signs brush marks in the snow where its wing tips touched down.   _____

14. Now we never walk in the snow without looking for sign of this northern visitor the white owl who brings silent death. _____

15. We heard Oliver give the commencement address at Bennington College in Bennington Vermont. _____

UNIT 11 Spelling

Hodges': chapter 18
Writer's: chapter 36

Everyone notices the sign that invites you to eat at the "Resturant" or the one that offers "Wood for Sell." And, right or wrong, most people tend to brand both the owner and the maker of such a sign as uneducated. There is simply no other error in composition that is so universally recognized and deplored as the misspelled word. Because of the stigma of illiteracy that it carries, misspelling should be the first and most important concern of any poor speller.

If you are a poor speller, one who regularly misspells enough words to have your class-work or professional work graded down, you should begin a definite program for improving your spelling skills. There are many excellent spelling manuals available today that make use of the latest psychological studies to present words in a logical, easy-to-learn order.

You may also find the following procedures helpful as you learn the rules of spelling presented in this section of the book.

Proofread your papers carefully at least once for misspelled words only. As you write a rough draft, it is often difficult, and always distracting, to look up a great number of words, but you can put a check or some other identifying sign above those words you have any doubts about so that you can look up their spelling when you proofread.

If you have difficulty spotting misspelled words in your own composition, try to slow down your reading of the rough draft by pointing to each word with a pencil. Or even read your writing from right to left instead of the usual left to right to be sure that you see individual words rather than groups of words. You need, whenever possible, to make more than two drafts of your paper because you will be unlikely to see your errors in a rough draft that has many words and phrases crossed through or that has barely legible handwriting.

Create for yourself a list of words you commonly misspell. Like most people you will tend to misspell certain words repeatedly, so you should review your own spelling list frequently to break your bad spelling habits.

A comparison of your spelling list with someone else's will usually show—surprisingly enough—only two or three words in common. The mastery of spelling is an individual matter, differing with each person. You get some benefit from mastering lists of frequently misspelled words, but your own individual spelling list is the all-important one for you.

Write the words you misspell by syllables; then write the definitions of the words; finally, use the words in sentences.

E NIG MAT IC

puzzling or baffling

[My boss's behavior toward me was *enigmatic* until she sat down and explained what she expected of me.]

AT TRIB UTE

as a noun, an object or quality that belongs to or represents someone or something

[The *attributes* of Santa Claus have been expanded over the years.]

On the following pages are rules that will help you to avoid misspelling many common words. Following the explanation of each rule is an exercise to reinforce the rule in your mind.

Adding Prefixes

Name_____ **Score** _____

Add the prefix to the root word without doubling or adding letters. (The root is the base word to which the prefix or suffix is added.) Notice that adding the prefix changes the meaning of the root word.

un-   +   necessary   =   unnecessary

mis-   +   spell   =   misspell

dis-   +   agree   =   disagree

DIRECTIONS In the blank at the right enter the correct spelling of each word with the prefix added. Consult your dictionary freely. Some dictionaries hyphenate some of the following words.

EXAMPLES

mis-   +   quote   *misquote*_____

pre-   +   eminent   *preeminent*_____

1. dis-   +   satisfied   _____

2. dis-   +   appear   _____

3. mis-   +   pronounce   _____

4. mis-   +   understand _____

5. mis-   +   step   _____

6. un-   +   noticed   _____

7. un-   +   usual   _____

8. dis-   +   approve   _____

9. dis-   +   similar   _____

10. mis- +   spent   _____

11. mis- +   behave   _____

12. dis- +   able   _____

13. mis- +   interpret   _____

14. re-   +   take   _____

15. re-   +   evaluate   _____

Adding Suffixes—Final *e*

Name_____ Score _____

Drop the final *e* before a suffix beginning with a vowel but not before a suffix beginning with a consonant.

bride	+	-al	=	bridal	fame	+	-ous	=	famous
care	+	-ful	=	careful	entire	+	-ly	=	entirely

Exceptions: due, duly; awe, awful; hoe, hoeing; singe, singeing. After *c* or *g* the final *e* is retained before suffixes beginning with *a* or *o: notice, noticeable; courage, courageous.*

DIRECTIONS With the aid of your dictionary, write the correct spelling of each word with the suffix added. Write (*ex*) after each answer that is an exception to rule.

EXAMPLES

argue	+	-ing	*arguing*
dye	+	-ing	*dying*

1. become	+	-ing	_____
2. use	+	-age	_____
3. hope	+	-ing	_____
4. excite	+	-able	_____
5. drive	+	-ing	_____
6. outrage	+	-ous	_____
7. like	+	-ly	_____
8. write	+	-ing	_____
9. advise	+	-able	_____
10. arrange	+	-ment	_____
11. value	+	-able	_____
12. manage	+	-ment	_____
13. advantage	+	-ous	_____
14. judge	+	-ment	_____
15. extreme	+	-ly	_____

Adding Suffixes—Doubling the Consonant   Exercise 11-3

Name_____ **Score** _____

When the suffix begins with a vowel (*ing, ed, ence, ance, able*), double a final single consonant if it is preceded by a single vowel and is in an accented syllable. (A word of one syllable, of course, is always accented.)

mop, mo**pp**ed   [compare with *mope, moped*]

mop, mo**pp**ing   [compare with *mope, moping*]

con·fer´, con·fer´red   [final consonant in the accented syllable]

ben´e·fit; ben´e·fited   [final consonant not in the accented syllable]

need, needed   [final consonant not preceded by a single vowel]

DIRECTIONS In the blank at the right enter the correct spelling of each word with the suffix added. Consult your dictionary freely.

EXAMPLE

control   +   -ed   *controlled* _____

1. stop   +   -ing   _____
2. occur   +   -ing   _____
3. pour   +   -ing   _____
4. proceed   +   -ed   _____
5. unforget +   -able   _____
6. begin   +   -ing   _____
7. control   +   -able   _____
8. transmit +   -ing   _____
9. equip   +   -ed   _____
10. meet   +   -ing   _____
11. prefer   +   -ed   _____
12. big   +   -est   _____
13. push   +   -ed   _____
14. fat   +   -er   _____
15. attach   +   -ed   _____

Copyright © 2004 Heinle

Adding Suffixes—Final *y*

Name_____ **Score** _____

Except before *ing,* final *y* preceded by a consonant is changed to *i* before a suffix.

| defy | + | -ance | = | defiance | happy | + | -ness | = | happiness |
| modify | + | -er | = | modifier | modify | + | -ing | = | modifying |

To make a noun plural or a verb singular, final *y* preceded by a consonant is changed to *i* and *es* is added.

| duty | + | -es | = | duties | deny | + | -es | = | denies |
| ally | + | -es | = | allies | copy | + | -es | = | copies |

Final *y* preceded by a vowel is usually not changed before a suffix.

| annoy | + | -ed | = | annoyed | turkey | + | -s | = | turkeys |

Exceptions: pay, paid; lay, laid; say, said; day, daily

DIRECTIONS With the aid of your dictionary, enter the correct spelling of each word with the suffix added. Write (*ex*) after each word that is an exception to rule.

EXAMPLE

| boundary | + | -es | *boundaries* |
| pay | + | -d | *paid (ex)* |

1. monkey	+	-s	_____
2. try	+	-es	_____
3. accompany	+	-es	_____
4. chimney	+	-s	_____
5. bury	+	-ed	_____
6. lay	+	-ed	_____
7. fallacy	+	-es	_____
8. hungry	+	-ly	_____
9. lonely	+	-ness	_____
10. donkey	+	-s	_____

Suffixes—Forming the Plural

Name_____ **Score** _____

Form the plural of most nouns by (1) adding *s* to the singular form of the noun, (2) adding *es* to singular nouns ending in *s, ch, sh,* and *x,* or (3) changing the *y* to *i* and adding *es* if the noun ends in a *y* preceded by a consonant.

boy ⟶ boys	fox ⟶ foxes	mystery ⟶ mysteries
cupful ⟶ cupfuls	Harris ⟶ Harrises	beauty ⟶ beauties
Drehmel ⟶ Drehmels	genius ⟶ geniuses	reply ⟶ replies

A few nouns change their form for the plural: *woman ⟶ women; child ⟶ children*. And a few nouns ending in *o* take the *es* plural: *potato ⟶ potatoes; hero ⟶ heroes*. And a few nouns change an *f* to a *v* and add *s* or *es: calf ⟶ calves; knife ⟶ knives*.

DIRECTIONS In the blank enter the plural form of each word. Consult your dictionary freely.

EXAMPLES

day *days*

scratch *scratches*

1. speech _____
2. box _____
3. industry _____
4. veto _____
5. wolf _____
6. radio _____
7. witch _____
8. scientist _____
9. address _____
10. city _____

11. question _____
12. ghetto _____
13. article _____
14. leaf _____
15. watch _____
16. man _____
17. professor _____
18. business _____
19. Jones _____
20. army _____

Confusion of *ie* and *ei*

Name_____ **Score** _____

When the sound is *ee* (as in *see*), write *ei* after *c* (*receipt, ceiling*), and *ie* after any other letter (*relieve, priest*); when the sound is other than *ee*, usually write *ei* (*eight, their, reign*).

Exceptions: either, neither, financier, leisure, seize, species, weird

Note: This rule does not apply when *ei* or *ie* is not pronounced as one simple sound (*alien, audience, fiery*) or when *cie* stands for *sh* (*ancient, conscience, efficient*).

DIRECTIONS With the aid of your dictionary, fill in the blanks in the following words by writing *ei* or *ie*. Write (*ex*) after any word that is an exception to the rule.

EXAMPLES

dec_____*ei*_____ve

_____*ei*_____ther

1. rec_____ve
2. bel_____s
3. ch_____f
4. s_____ge
5. conc_____ted
6. y_____ld
7. gr_____f
8. l_____sure
9. misch_____f
10. sl_____gh

11. th_____f
12. gr_____ve
13. spec_____s
14. w_____ght
15. c_____ling
16. rel_____ve
17. h_____ght
18. f_____nd
19. n_____ther
20. f_____ld

Homonyms and Homophones

Name_____   *Score* _____

Distinguish between words that differ in meaning but have a similar sound and/or spelling, such as *lose-loose* and *to-too-two*.

DIRECTIONS In the following sentences, cross out the spelling or spellings in parentheses that do not fit the meaning, and write the correct spelling in the blank. Consult your dictionary freely.

EXAMPLE

We are (~~holey~~, wholly, ~~holy~~) committed to our new mayor's plans to revive the downtown square.
wholly

1. As we (herd, heard) his plans, we applauded.
_____

2. From a few pessimists there immediately came the (prophesy, prophecy) that he would never succeed.
_____

3. But the general (affect, effect) of his announcement was positive.
_____

4. Those of us who had lived (through, threw) the previous mayor's administration felt vindicated.
_____

5. He had managed to (loose, lose) federal matching funds for the revival of the area.
_____

6. There were other (instances, instants) of a lack of business acumen.
_____

7. Now we are using a photograph of the restored courthouse as a logo on our (stationary, stationery).
_____

8. All the downtown merchants (except, accept) one have committed to the restoration.
_____

9. And two architects have offered to provide free (counsel, council) as the merchants plan their futures.
_____

10. Of more immediate concern is (advise, advice) about discovering the history of each building.
_____

11. The downtown (site, cite, sight) should preserve local history.
_____

12. Anyone who has (ideals, ideas) to contribute should contact us by next Friday.
_____

13. Our (principal, principle) concern is preventing people from making changes before they plan carefully.
_____

14. We believe a restored downtown will raise the (moral, morale) of everyone.   _____

15. All of us are (conscience, conscious) of our obligation to the public.   _____

Hyphenation

Name_____ **Score** _____

In general, use the hyphen (1) between two or more words serving as a single adjective before a noun, (2) with compound numbers from twenty-one to ninety-nine and with spelled-out fractions, (3) with prefixes or suffixes for clarity, (4) with the prefixes *ex-, self-, all-*, and *great-* and the suffix *elect,* and (5) between a prefix and a proper name.

(1) a *know-it-all* expression

(2) *sixty-six, one-half*

(3) *re-collect* the supplies (to distinguish from recollect an event)

(4) *ex-wife, self-help, all-important, great-grandmother, mayor-elect*

(5) *mid-July, un-American*

DIRECTIONS Supply hyphens where they are needed in the following list. Not all items require hyphens.

EXAMPLES

a well-spent childhood

a childhood well spent

1. a long distance call

2. a four foot barricade

3. a twenty five year old coach

4. ex President Bush

5. President elect Walker

6. a high rise apartment

7. a commonly used adjective

8. chocolate covered cherries

9. students who are career minded

10. the all seeing eye of the camera

11. a two thirds vote of the senate

12. Two thirds of the senate approved.

13. western style jeans

14. the clumsily executed dance

15. He is forty five.

16. She is my great aunt.

17. an all inclusive study

18. results that are long lasting

19. long lasting results

20. My small daughter is amazingly self sufficient.

21. The officer re searched the suspect.

22. a two part answer

23. The answer had two parts

24. The up and down motion of the roller coaster made her ill.

25. The shop specializes in young people's fashions.

26. I feel good as gold today.

27. We are all ready to go.

28. a win at any cost attitude

29. in mid December

30. a walk-in closet

UNIT 12

Capitalization

Hodges': chapter 9
Writer's: chapter 37

Proper names and acronyms

Capitalize proper names and words used as essential parts of proper names.

Persons	Shakespeare, Buddha, Mr. White
Personifications	Mother Nature, Uncle Sam, John Doe
Places	Key West; LaGrange, Georgia; Byron Avenue; the South (referred to as an area)
Things	the Liberty Bell, the Bible, History 201, the Second World War
Times	Wednesday, April 14; Easter; The Age of Enlightenment
Organizations	the Peace Corps, the Exchange Club, Phi Beta Kappa
Races and Languages	Oriental, English, Latin
Religions and Their Adherents	Islam, Christianity, Judaism, Moslem, Christian, Jew
Holy Books and Holy Days	Koran, the Bible, Torah, Ramadan, Advent, Passover
Words Denoting the Supreme Being	Allah, God, Jehovah
Words Derived from Proper Names	Swedish, New Yorker, Anglican
Essential Parts of Proper Names	the Bill of Rights, the Battle of Little Big Horn, the New River

Titles of rank or address

In general, capitalize a person's title if it immediately precedes the person's name but not a title that follows the name.

> In the last election, **R**epresentative Andrew Nunnery faced Rachel Lavery, former governor, in the race for senator.

Note that usage varies with regard to capitalization of titles of high rank when not followed by a proper name (Senator OR senator). Titles of family members are capitalized only when they are written in combination with a name (Uncle Ben) or when they are used in place of a name (I asked Father for a loan.).

Titles and subtitles

Capitalize the first and last words of a title or subtitle and all other key words within it.

> A writer friend of mine suggested that I read two articles: "**W**hat's a **Z**ip **D**rive **F**or?" and "**H**ow to **T**weak **Y**our **V**ideo **C**ard."

Caution: Articles—*a, an, the*—and prepositions, coordinating conjunctions, and the *to* in infinitives are not capitalized unless they are the first or last words.

First words of sentences and of directly quoted speech

Capitalize the first word of each sentence, including a quoted sentence.

> Writers agree that many good novels were rejected by publishers last year.
>
> OR
>
> "Writers agree that many good novels were rejected by publishers last year," Ms. Chiu explained.
>
> "Oh, really!" exclaimed a student.

Unnecessary capitals

Avoid capitalizing words that name classes rather than specific persons, places, and things.

> The **d**octors held a **c**onference at a **c**onvention **c**enter in the **d**owntown section of our town.

Also avoid the common tendency to capitalize seasons, directions, and general courses of study.

> This spring I am going to study **c**hemistry at a **w**estern university.

Capitals

Name_____ Score _____

DIRECTIONS Words in one of each of the following groups should be capitalized. Identify the group that needs capitalization by writing either *a* or *b* in the blank at right. Then make the necessary revision for the appropriate group of words.

EXAMPLE

    (a) a class at our college   _____

                B   M   C

    (b) geology at bryn mawr college   ___b___

1. (a) responded, "you will see me again."   _____

    (b) responded that you will see me again   _____

2. (a) a course in history   _____

    (b) a course in latin   _____

3. (a) visited another country during the holiday   _____

    (b) visited mexico during the christmas holiday   _____

4. (a) the bill of rights and constitution   _____

    (b) equal rights and amendments   _____

5. (a) boarded the queen mary for its last crossing of the atlantic   _____

    (b) boarded an ocean liner for its last transoceanic voyage   _____

6. (a) a story in a weekly magazine about the death of a popular rock singer   _____

    (b) "the tragedy of the king's last years," a story in newsweek about the death of elvis   _____

7. (a) representative gordon visiting tennessee   _____

    (b) the representative from our state   _____

8. (a) admired the painting by the artist   _____

    (b) admired les demoiselles by picasso   _____

9. (a) the pronunciation of the word party as "pah-ty" in the south   _____

    (b) the pronunciation of words in a southern state   _____

10. (a) a famous war in history   _____

    (b) the war of 1812   _____

11. (a) went to see a well-known play during our annual trip to a
       neighboring city   _____

    (b) went to see the musical into the woods during our annual trip
        to new york   _____

12. (a) the president of our country will be inaugurated on tuesday,
        january 20   _____

    (b) the president of a social club at our college   _____

13. (a) keats' courting of death in la belle dame sans merci   _____

    (b) the many poems that personify human qualities   _____

14. (a) economics 211 to be offered in the spring   _____

    (b) a course in economics to be offered in the spring   _____

15. (a) the grandmother who joined a charitable organization   _____

    (b) my chinese grandmother who is a red cross volunteer   _____

UNIT 13

Italics

Hodges': chapter 10
Writer's: chapter 38

To show italics, underline the titles of books, films, plays, works of art, magazines, newspapers, and long poems; the names of ships and airplanes; foreign words; and words, letters, and figures spoken of as such.

The word *modern* becomes important when you consider these works of art: Proust's novel *Remembrance of Things Past;* Modigliani's inspiring sculpture *Flight;* Matisse's masterpiece painted in 1906, *Le Bonheur de Vivre;* and even a work of engineering such as the *Golden Gate Bridge.*

Titles of plays, books, and other long works

Use italics to identify the titles of separate publications.

Books	*Remembrance of Rivers Past*
Magazines	*Computer Shopper, Fine Woodworking*
Newspapers	*Manchester Guardian, San Francisco Chronicle*
Plays, Films	*Death of a Salesman, A River Runs Through It*
Recordings	*I Heard It Through the Grape Vine, Sheherazade*
Works of Art	Michelangelo's *David,* Winslow Homer's *Corn Husking*
Long Poems	*Beowulf,* William Wordsworth's *The Prelude*
Comic Strips	*Janis and Arlo, Dilbert*
Genera Species	*Anas platyrhynchos* (genus and species of the mallard duck)
Software	*Myst, Norton Utilities*

Caution: Do not underline the title of your own essay or overuse italics for emphasis.

Foreign words

Use italics to identify foreign words and phrases in the context of an English sentence.

> In this portrait she sits on a *tatami* mat wearing a *kosode*. . . . Toys are by her side, including a papier-mâché dog, a top, and dolls, as well as an incense container. (From a description of an artifact in an exhibit of Japanese Daimyo culture at the National Gallery of Art)

Names of legal cases, ships, satellites, and spacecraft

Sputnik   *Roe v. Wade*

Galileo space probe   *U.S.S. Constitution*

Words, letters, and numbers spoken of as such in a sentence

> "We have designated Larry as the Alpha Geek," announced David. "He now will sign his name with the figure *ΑΓ*."

Emphasized words

Use italics sparingly to indicate emphasis.

> If Father accepts the offer, he will be *your* problem, not mine.

Italics

Name_____ Score _____

DIRECTIONS Words in one of each of the following groups should be italicized (underlined). Identify the group that needs italicizing by writing either *a* or *b* in the blank at right. Then make the necessary revision for the appropriate group of words.

EXAMPLE

(a) reading the newspaper's lead story _____

(b) reading the lead story in the <u>Times-Picayune</u>   *b*_____

1. (a) our next one-act play, Don't Go There _____

   (b) our next play one-act play _____

2. (a) the landmark case on free speech _____

   (b) the landmark case, Rienart v. Cobb _____

3. (a) Han Solo's starship _____

   (b) Han Solo's starship, the Millenium Falcon _____

4. (a) reading The Stone Diaries _____

   (b) reading a novel about relationships _____

5. (a) the flight of whooping cranes _____

   (b) the flight of whooping cranes (Grus Americana) _____

6. (a) a story in a weekly magazine about the death of a popular rock singer _____

   (b) "the tragedy of the king's last years," an essay in Newsweek about the death of Elvis _____

7. (a) the essay in the journal for college English teachers _____

   (b) the essay in the journal College English _____

8. (a) admired the painting by the artist _____

   (b) admired The Singing Fish by Joan Miró _____

9. (a) a book made into a movie by Robert Redford _____

   (b) the book A River Runs Through It _____

10. (a) a famous statue _____

    (b) Michelangelo's David _____

11. (a) went to see a well-known play during our vacation   _____

    (b) went to see Noises Off during our vacation in London   _____

12. (a) Warf chose the antique Klingon sword   _____

    (b) Warf chose the S'harien   _____

13. (a) Larry's favorite kind of sushi   _____

    (b) the tekka don on the menu   _____

14. (a) the best utility software   _____

    (b) the newest version of Norton Antivirus   _____

15. (a) the guru of management theory   _____

    (b) Dogbert's management theory as expressed in Dilbert   _____

UNIT 14

Abbreviations, Acronyms, and Numbers

Hodges': chapter 11
Writer's: chapter 39

In specialized kinds of writing—such as tables, indexes, and footnotes—abbreviations, acronyms, and figures are appropriate; but in ordinary writing abbreviations are used sparingly, figures are used only for numbers that would require three or more words to write out, and acronyms should be spelled out the first time they are used.

Titles of address or position

Before proper names, use the abbreviations *Mr., Mrs., Ms., Dr.,* and *St.* (for Saint) as appropriate. Use such designations as *Jr., Sr., II,* and *Ph.D.* after a proper name.

Ms. Dean asked *Dr.* Bray to tell the story of *St.* Jude.

Names of countries, continents, states, months

Spell out names of states, countries, continents, months, days of week, and units of measurement.

When Claudia was born on *July 8* at the hospital in Barcelona, *Spain,* she weighed six *pounds, eleven ounces;* but seven days later, at home in Sierra City, *California,* she weighed nine *pounds.*

Abbreviations in addresses

Spell out *Street, Road, Park, River, Company,* and similar words when used as part of proper names.

From London *Avenue* in Riverview *Park* you can see the Stones *River* and the Collier Realty *Company*.

Abbreviations for parts of books and reference materials

Spell out the words *volume, chapter,* and *page* and the names of courses of study.

> The notes on *chemistry* are taken from *volume* 1, *chapter* 7, *page* 63. [*Vol.* 1, *Ch.* 7, *p.* 63 would be acceptable in a footnote.]

Recognize the meanings of several common Latin expressions, which are usually spelled out in English in formal writing.

> *i.e.* [that is], *e.g.* [for example], *viz.* [formerly]

> *cf.* [compare], *etc.* [and so forth], *vs.* OR *v.* [versus]

Caution: Never write *and etc.*, and use the word *etc.* itself sparingly. In general, naming another item is more effective.

> This course covers southern literature, history, geography, demographics, and food.

> [Naming another item, *food*, is more effective than writing *etc.*]

Acronyms

Spell out the meaning of any acronym that may not be familiar to your reader when you use it for the first time.

> The NTSB (National Transportation Safety Board) is investigating the crash.

Numbers

Spell out numbers that require only one or two words, but use figures for other numbers.

> After twenty-five years of my wife's wonderful cooking, I have gone from a *twenty-nine* inch waist to a *thirty-six* inch waist.

> Our home covers *2500* square feet.

Note the ways numerals are used in the following instances:

(1) the hour of the day: 4:00 P.M. (p.m.) or four o'clock in the afternoon

(2) dates: April *14, 1992*

(3) addresses: *1310* West Main

(4) identification numbers: Channel *27,* Interstate *81*

(5) pages or divisions of a book: page *87,* chapter *9*

(6) decimals and percentages: *.87* inches, *10* percent

(7) a series of numbers: a room *20* feet long, *12* feet wide, and *8* feet high; The vote was *19* to *4* in favor with 7 abstentions.

(8) large round numbers: two million light years

(9) at the beginning of the sentence: One hundred fifty people applied for the position.

Abbreviations, Acronyms, and Numbers

Name_____ Score _____

DIRECTIONS Rewrite each of the following items using an abbreviation or a figure if the abbreviation or the figure would be appropriate in ordinary writing. If not, simply rewrite the item as it stands.

EXAMPLES

three o'clock in the afternoon

3:00 p.m.

on Tuesday afternoon

on Tuesday afternoon

1. on page fifteen of chapter three

2. fourteen thousand dollars

3. Jim Nunnery, the doctor on our street

4. the Braves vs. the Yankees

5. Eighty percent of those registered voted.

6. debate about the Equal Rights Amendment

7. life in California in nineteen ninety-two

8. the economics class in Peck Hall

9. one hundred pounds

10. on the twenty-first of January

11. Riverview Park off Thompson lane

12. Bonnie Jones, our senator

13. John White, a certified public accountant

14. between the United States and Canada

15. a lot that is one hundred feet long and ninety-five feet wide with seventy-five feet of road frontage

PART 3

Word Selection and Word Use

UNIT 15

Usage

Hodges': chapter 19
Writer's: chapter 28

Appropriate to audience

Specialists in specific subject matter often use a technical language in their communications with each other. For example, a chemist might write this sentence with another chemist in mind as the reader: **In this molecule we have also replaced the dimerization module with a non-dimerizing synthetic linker.** A general reader, however, will have no idea what the technical terms mean.

Jargon is a similarly confusing technical language tailored for a particular occupation. For example a NASCAR driver or worker may use these terms freely: **chicane, Darlington stripes, dirty air, flat spot.** Although a general reader can imagine a context in which some of the terms might make sense, the reader will not know the meaning that they hold for the NASCAR specialist.

Clearly, then, a writer will wish to avoid technical language and jargon when writing to a general reader unless such terms efficiently explain a concept and can be defined within the context of the writing.

When we consider our readers as we write, we also become mindful of using inclusive language, language that is not sexist and does not treat men and women differently. For example, many readers believe that using the term *men* to refer to both men and women excludes women. Writers also should avoid stereotyping sex roles—for example assuming that all doctors are men and all nurses are women.

Easily confused words

Be careful to distinguish between verbs with similar spellings like *sit/set, lie/lay,* and *rise/raise.* Remember that *sit, lie,* and *rise* cannot take objects, but *set, lay,* and *raise* can.

                                           object
While Diana *sat* in her favorite chair, Rucker *laid out* several books for her to read and
object
raised the television to a comfortable viewing level.

The books *were set* on a nearby table.

Notice in the second example above that the word you expect to be the object of set—that is, *books*—is made the subject of the sentence. Thus the subject of the sentence is not acting but is being acted upon. In such a case, the verb is said to be passive.

The verbs *set, lay,* and *raise* can be made passive, but the verbs *sit, lie,* and *rise* cannot because they cannot take objects.

The books were *set* down.   [NOT *sat* down]

The books were *laid* down.   [NOT *lain* down]

The television was *raised*.   [NOT was *risen*]

Of these six difficult verbs, the most troublesome combination is *lie/lay* because the past-tense form of *lie* is *lay.*

He *lays* out the books and then *lies* down to rest.

After he had *laid* out the books, he *lay* down to rest.

Be careful to add the *-d* or *-ed* ending to the past and perfect tenses of verbs like *use* and to verbs that end in *-k* or *-t.*

He has use*d* only ten minutes of his nap time.

She ask*ed* for her copy of Beth Henley's *Crimes of the Heart*.

Sit/Set, Lie/Lay, Rise/Raise

Name _____ **Score** _____

DIRECTIONS Replace the italicized verbs in the following sentences with the appropriate form of *lie/lay, sit/set,* or *rise/raise.* Do not change the verb tense and be prepared to explain your revision.

EXAMPLE

The cat *lifts* the window blinds with her paw.

The cat raises the window blinds with her paw.

1. I *place* the cat on the windowsill.

2. *"Stay,"* I command her, as if she were a dog.

3. While she is *resting* on the windowsill, I work at my computer.

4. I am *putting* my books on the shelves above my monitor.

5. The cat *has rested* quietly for almost thirty minutes.

6. Soon she will decide *to nap* elsewhere.

7. I can *adjust* my watch according to her habits since she changes positions every thirty minutes.

8. She *leaves* her toys beside her when she sleeps.

9. During a conversation with my friends I *introduced* the issue of training the cat.

10. I could see the cat preparing to *stand* and walk away.

Appropriate Usage

Name_____ Score _____

DIRECTIONS In each sentence, choose the proper word or words from the pairs in parentheses. Cross out the incorrect word or words and write the correct one in the blank. Rely on your dictionary to help you choose the word with the correct meaning or the word that is appropriate in a formal essay.

EXAMPLE

(Alot, Lots of, Many) of us from Professor Hague's class will watch
Angel.   *Many*_____

1. We are (analyzing, synthesizing) the recurring themes of the
   series.   _____

2. We have been reading fiction and poetry by (various, varied)
   science fiction writers.   _____

3. My roommate Jenny was only (partly, partially) serious when she
   suggested *Buffy the Vampire Slayer* as a topic for discussion.   _____

4. (Surprisedly, Surprisingly) Dr. Hague agreed with Jenny.   _____

5. She told the class about a paper she is writing on Buffy for the
   (eminent, imminent) meeting of the Popular Culture Association.   _____

6. She also is (corroborating, collaborating) on a book about *The
   Sopranos*.   _____

7. In her article she discusses the (concurring, recurring) theme of
   "disrespecting the Bing" in *The Sopranos*.   _____

8. Dr. Hague explores the ways several characters have divided
   allegiances (among, between) Tony and other mob bosses.   _____

9. In the most recent episode Tony sits at night in his car outside
   the (civil, civic) auditorium as the rain blackens the street around
   his black vehicle.   _____

10. His mood is equally black as he contemplates the contentious
    (fractions, factions) within his own mob.   _____

11. Tony (meditates, mediates) on a situation that may already be
    beyond his control.   _____

12. At every turn someone (affronts, confronts) the dignity that Tony
    believes he has rightfully earned.   _____

13. Dr. Hague points out the similarity of this plot to the (ethic,
    ethnic) dilemma in a recent *Seinfeld*.   _____

14. There are mediators in *Seinfeld* episodes, but the disputes never
    seem to be (dissolved, resolved).   _____

15. Seinfeld ended as *The Sopranos* seems destined to end,
    (pragmatically, enigmatically) and with the viewers conflicted
    about the conclusion.   _____

UNIT 16

Exactness

Hodges': chapter 20
Writer's: chapter 29

Since the basic unit of communication is the word, you cannot write clearly and accurately unless you have built up a vocabulary of words to express your thoughts and feelings. Of the 500,000 entries in an unabridged dictionary, most college students can use no more than 15,000 in speaking and writing. Building a vocabulary, then, is a lifetime process. Usually the more people read, the more words they add to their recognition vocabularies. After they have seen the same words many times in different contexts, they add these words to their active vocabularies, the words they actually use in speaking and writing.

People who do not regularly read newspapers, magazines, and books often have few words to draw from whenever they speak or write. They may complain, "I know what I mean, but I can't put it into words." They may also say that some works by professional writers are "too hard to understand." The source of their difficulty in both writing and reading is an inadequate vocabulary.

You can begin now to increase your vocabulary by noticing the words you read in your course work and by looking up definitions of all the words whose meanings you do not know. Reading a difficult paragraph aloud sometimes emphasizes the words you are not familiar with and, as a result, helps you understand why the paragraph is difficult for you.

While you are increasing your recognition vocabulary, you must take great care to make the best possible use of the words in your active vocabulary.

Precise word choice

To express yourself exactly, you must choose the words that have the denotations (the definitions found in dictionaries) and the connotations (the mental or emotional associations that go with the words) that you intend.

Problem with   The failure of the movie was *contributed* to its being badly
Denotation   directed.

Correct Denotation	The failure of the movie was *attributed* to its being badly directed.
Problem with Connotation	I took my best friend to my *pad* for dinner.
Correct Connotation	I took my best friend to my *home* for dinner.

Remember that a wrong word is very noticeable when it results in a ridiculous sentence.

Wrong Word	Faust pledged his *sole* to the devil in exchange for power and knowledge.
Correct Word	Faust pledged his *soul* to the devil in exchange for power and knowledge.

Whenever possible you should choose concrete rather than abstract words. Abstract words refer to ideas, whereas concrete words refer to definite objects. Abstract words are necessary to state generalizations, but it is the specific word, the specific detail, the specific example that engages the reader's attention.

General	Gwen White described Lee Smith's story "Intensive Care" as interesting.
Specific	Gwen White described Lee Smith's story "Intensive Care" as her favorite portrayal of a man in mid-life crisis.
General	Gwen must write a lot if she is to finish her novel.
Specific	Gwen must write at least four pages each day for the next two months if she is to finish her novel before her deadline.

Idioms

You use idiomatic phrases every day without thinking about their meaning: "I ran across some old biology notes today" and "Sarah played down the importance of not balancing her checkbook." Native English speakers use expressions like these naturally; but some idioms may seem unnatural, even ridiculous, to foreigners trying to learn our language.

Even native speakers sometimes have difficulty choosing the correct prepositions to make expressions idiomatic. For example, many would write "prior than" rather than the idiomatic "prior to." The dictionary is the best guide for helping you choose the preposition that should follow a word like *prior* to make an idiomatic expression.

Unidiomatic	The citations in her research paper did not *comply to* MLA guidelines.
Idiomatic	The citations in her research paper did not *comply with* MLA guidelines.

Clichés

When idiomatic expressions have been used too much, they become trite—worn out and meaningless. At one time readers would have thought the expression "tried and true" was an exact and effective choice of words. But readers today have seen and heard the expression so often that they hardly notice it, except perhaps to be bored or amused by it. Clichés of this sort are common in most people's speech and may even occur at times in the work of professional writers, but they should be avoided because they no longer communicate ideas exactly. Beware also of political slogans, advertising jargon, and most slang expressions: they are often so overused for a brief period of time that they quickly become meaningless.

Trite	Last but not least is the dedicated student who rises at the crack of dawn to hit the books.
Exact	Last is the dedicated student who rises at 6:00 A.M. to study.

Exactness

Name_____ **Score** _____

DIRECTIONS To see how becoming aware of words in your reading can lead to a better recognition vocabulary, try this experiment. Read aloud the first paragraph below, underlining the words whose meaning you are uncertain of; then look up the definitions and write them down; finally, reread the sentences in which those words appear. When you have finished with the first paragraph, go on to the second one. Notice how the words that gave you trouble in the first paragraph seem to stand out in the second paragraph, though sometimes as a different part of speech or in a different tense. If you cannot remember the definitions of the words, look again at your notes.

PARAGRAPH 1

The lone man had been walking about Oxford, Mississippi, all day, and several residents had remarked on his presence. With his long unkempt hair, corduroy jacket, and satchel of books, he appeared to them to be the quintessential graduate student or aspiring young writer. The owner of the corner store, a resident for over forty years, said he reminded him of a young Sherwood Anderson or Sinclair Lewis. He had spoken with the young man and reported him to be polite and intense with an aseptic smile. He had asked for directions to Faulkner's grave, so that confirmed him as a writer, though not a writer manqué. As night fell the young writer made his way to Faulkner's grave and knelt beside it. He took from his satchel what they later found to be a mantilla and left it on the grave enfolding a marcescent rose.

PARAGRAPH 2

The wreath over the mantle contains marcescent roses and blue bells. It smells faintly of bay leaves and salty air. They brought it back from a trip to New Orleans, the quintessential four-day vacation after a week of intense pressure at work. Avoiding Bourbon Street, they visited several old Catholic churches, he in his chinos and chambray shirts, she with a delicate lace mantilla over her head. Someone in each church greeted them warmly and invited them to stay for service. They responded with compliments to the architecture and aseptic smiles. When they returned from the trip, the neighbors asked about it politely over the neatly trimmed privet hedge. They responded with comments about the weather and aseptic smiles. Their marriage, as well they know, is a marriage manqué, a failure not of tragic proportions, just a sad and unhappy union.

Exactness

Name _____ Score _____

DIRECTIONS The following sentences all employ idioms, many of which are also clichés. Rewrite the sentences so they are clear and not idiomatic.

EXAMPLE

The instructions for completing this assignment are wishy-washy.

The instructions for completing this assignment are unclear.

1. I would just as soon use the PC as the Mac for our project.

2. I used to go to the grill every evening to chill.

3. I knew that sooner or later I would need to listen up to coach and stop trash talking while the quarterback calls a play.

4. It is raining cats and dogs tonight, but I am working at the computer.

5. I pulled an all-nighter for a history exam last night, so I need help focusing today.

6. We need an Internet-related topic, one that is on the cutting edge, one that will make Professor Blackwell say, "Too cool!"

7. Aleka has kept her nose to the grindstone and has kept her eye out for a good topic.

8. We know Professor Blackwell will jump all over us tomorrow if we don't have a rough draft.

9. Aleka says we should write about nano-technology, but Claudia and Angela say we should do a topic that people can wrap their brains around.

10. I guess at the eleventh hour when we have beaten our brains out over this, we will find a topic and write a rough draft.

UNIT 17

Conciseness

Hodges': chapter 21
Writer's: chapter 30

Almost every writer's first draft includes many words that are not needed and lacks some words that are. Only a careful revision based on close proofreading can transform a rough draft into an effective piece of writing.

Rough draft with revisions:

~~At this point in the semester it is the thinking of~~ T^he class ~~that we~~ want^ to see two of Beth Henley's plays. ~~First we want to see~~ *Crimes of the Heart.* ~~Then we want to see~~ *and* *Miss Firecracker.* ~~We thought about seeing *Am I Blue,* but we decided not to. That opinion has been seconded by~~ our teacher Ms^O Dunkerley. ~~She agrees,~~ ~~that we should see *Crimes of the Heart* and *Miss Firecracker.*~~ F^ortunately the local theatre group is doing ~~both plays.~~ *and* *f* *and June and* ~~They are doing~~ *Crimes of the Heart* in May. ~~In April they will do~~ *Miss Firecracker.* *in June.*

Wordiness

Use one clear word instead of a long phrase whenever possible. Following is a list of some more common wordy phrases and their one-word counterparts.

Wordy	Concise
to be desirous of	want or desire
to have a preference for	prefer
to be in agreement with	agree
due to the fact that	because
in view of the fact that	because or since
in order to	to
at this point in time	now

Copyright © 2004 Heinle

207

Wordy	Concise
in this day and age	today
with reference to	about
prior to	before
in the event of	if

Another kind of wordiness results from the writer's lack of confidence in his/her position. Such wordiness frequently includes expressions like "I think," "it seems to me," "in my opinion," and "would be."

Wordy	In my opinion the best starting point for discussion of the play would be Meg's relationship to her father.
Concise	Discussion of the play should start with Meg's relationship to her father.

Wordiness may also be caused by sentences that begin with *there* or *it*. To eliminate this kind of wordiness, restructure your sentences to use an active verb in place of the form of *to be* that inevitably follows *there* or *is*.

Wordy	There are two plays that we will discuss—*Crimes of the Heart* and *Am I Blue*.
Concise	We will discuss two plays—*Crimes of the Heart* and *Am I Blue*.
Wordy	It is also true that we saw both plays performed on Broadway.
Concise	We saw both plays performed on Broadway

Combining sentences through subordination often eliminates wordiness.

Wordy	In *Crimes of the Heart* Babe shoots her husband. Her husband has caught her having an affair.
Concise	In *Crimes of the Heart* Babe shoots her husband who has caught her having an affair.
	[The *who* clause subordinates one idea.]
Wordy	Lenny's only male friend is Charlie. She stops seeing him. She is afraid to admit she is unable to have children.
Concise	Lenny's only male friend is Charlie whom she stops seeing because she is afraid to admit she can't have children.
	[The *whom* clause subordinates one idea, and the *because* clause subordinates a second idea and clarifies causality.]

Needless repetition

Repetition of the same word or idea in several consecutive sentences results in monotonous writing. Careful use of pronouns helps as much as anything to avoid this problem.

| Repetitious | Claudia's friend Julie has gone to New York to interview Henley. Julie will use the interview in her article on Henley. |
| Concise | Claudia's friend Julie, who has gone to New York to interview Henley, will use the interview in her article on Henley. |

Note: Several popular expressions are always repetitious: *each and every, any and all, various and sundry, if and when, combine together, revert back.* Other such expressions include *red in color, triangular in shape,* and *City of Roanoke.*

Repetitious	Each and every day we have a quiz on the novel.
Concise	Each day we have a quiz on the novel.
Repetitious	We will have a total of twenty quiz grades after next week.
Concise	We will have twenty quiz grades after next week.

In writing direct quotations, many students tend to overwork forms of the verb *say.* Remember that many verbs besides *said* can introduce direct quotations. *Explained, pointed out, noted, continued, described,* and *observed* are only a few.

| Repetitious | Ms. Swann said, "The quiz grades will count as one-fourth of your semester grade." She later said, "The three essays will count as the other three-fourths of the final grade." |
| Concise | Ms. Swann explained, "The quiz grades will count as one-fourth of your semester grade." She later added, "The three essays will count as the other three-fourths of the final grade." |

Necessary repetition

Repetition is useful when it improves emphasis, clarity, or coherence. Notice the effect of the repeated "every" in the following sentence.

Claudia sees *every* live performance, meets *every* actor, and interviews *every* playwright at our week-long Festival of Plays.

Wordiness and Needless Repetition | Exercise 17-1

Name_____ **Score** _____

DIRECTIONS Cross out needless words in each of the following sentences. For each sentence needing only that revision, write *1* in the blank; for sentences that need additional changes, even changes in punctuation, write *2* in the blank and make the needed revision. There may be more than one way to revise some sentences.

EXAMPLES

~~It can be clearly seen that~~ Shane Cleaveland's novel *Cold Trails* is autobiographical. _____*1*_____

His mother ~~likes it for that reason. She~~ says the novel ~~it~~ is her favorite*for that reason.* _____*2*_____

1. The main reason why the novel has gained a wide audience is its honest portrayal of a boy's maturation. _____

2. Cleaveland explained his ideas for the novel. He said it started as a simple story of a boy and his two hunting dogs. The two dogs are named Trailer and Tina. They are pointers. _____

3. When he was in town, he was interviewed by a local reporter. He told the reporter that the story complicated itself by bringing in an old man. His name is Elton. _____

4. In various and sundry ways Elton's relationship with the boy becomes the focus of the plot. _____

5. The plot needed complications. It needed something to cause the boy to think and learn. _____

6. A good plot must have, in my opinion, a complication. It adds interest because of the conflict. _____

7. The relationship of Elton and the boy is interesting. It is interesting primarily because Elton becomes a guide to the boy, a mentor. _____

8. Elton lives alone. He has been alone since he lost his wife to cancer after a few years of marriage. _____

9. The boy loves training his dogs in the fields. He wants to train his dogs to compete in field trials. _____

10. He meets Elton one day when he and the two pups are walking a trail beside Whitewater Creek. They are following the trail to the river. _____

11. Elton has set out poles to catch catfish. He has returned to check the poles. _____

12. The boy stands back and waits to be recognized. He waits for Felix to check the bait on each pole. _____

13. The sun is beginning to set. Its red glow casts a strange light as one pole slowly is pulled completely under water. _____

14. Shadows blacken the water. Even darker shadows dart under the surface. The shadows make the boy think fearsome thoughts. _____

15. The boy lays down his pack. He helps the old man. _____

16. The boy who is shy and retiring and seldom talks or speaks remains quiet. _____

17. He grabs the pole. He immediately feels the power of the huge fish. He knows he cannot hold on long. _____

18. Elton reaches in his bag (he had dropped it beside him) and brings out a small homemade gaff. _____

19. The boy hangs over the bank and reaches into the black water. The boy is small and frail. _____

20. He stands with great effort. A huge blue catfish hangs from his gaff. _____

UNIT 18

Clarity and Completeness

Hodges': chapter 22
Writer's: chapter 23

Confusion caused by omitted articles, verbs or their auxiliaries, or prepositions

Be careful to include all necessary articles, pronouns, conjunctions, and prepositions. Revised omissions are indicated by a caret (∧) in the following examples.

Include a needed article before a noun or another adjective.

In general, viewers find Buffy to be ∧ charming and ∧ inspiring character.
a   *an*

[The article *a* precedes a word that begins with a consonant; *an* precedes a word that begins with a vowel.]

Include necessary prepositions or conjunctions.

Buffy is the protagonist in a type ∧ program that appeals to nearly all viewers.
of

[*Type* is not an adjective here.]

Viewers believe ∧ and care for Buffy.
in

[*Believe for* is not idiomatic phrasing.]

Do not omit *that* when it is needed as a subordinating conjunction.

The show's creators realize ∧ Buffy must be a sympathetic character if she is to attract and hold viewers.
that

[*That* introduces the clause that functions as the complement of the sentence.]

David Lavery, a "Buffy, the Vampire Slayer" scholar, says ∧ Buffy's viewers regard her as a role model.
that

[Here the conjunction *that* signals the beginning of an indirect quotation.]

That may be omitted when the meaning of the sentence would be clear at first reading without it.

Lavery believes Buffy is an important cultural icon.

Include necessary verbs and helping verbs.

For several years now Lavery has *written* and will continue to write important books about television and movies.

[*Has continue to write* is an error in verb construction.]

Complete comparisons

Include all words necessary to complete a comparison.

The Popular Culture Festival is as successful *as* or more successful than any other local cultural event.

Most Americans know more about television than *about* any other cultural medium.

Complete intensifiers

When used as intensifiers, *so, such,* and *too* should usually be followed by a completing phrase or clause.

There is **so** much going on at the Popular Culture Festival this year that I can hardly choose what to attend.

Lavery's session was **too** popular, so we had to move it to a larger hall.

Clarity and Completeness

Name_____ Score _____

DIRECTIONS In the following sentences, insert the words that are needed to make the meaning or the grammatical construction complete. In the blank, write the words that you have added.

EXAMPLE

                of
A wedding is a rite passage.   _____*of*_____
            ^

1. Wedding photos help us see the symbolic nature of weddings in collective lives.   _____

2. American couples have and will continue to pay huge prices for photograph albums of their weddings.   _____

3. Scholars report 84% of the couples will opt for traditional weddings.   _____

4. Despite the many changes in wedding rituals and the expectations of couples, most couples still want a set of photographs that portray the wedding as ideal.   _____

5. Of course, the photographs present the perfect image "conjugal bliss."   _____

6. Professional wedding photographers know that couples do not purchase less perfect images.   _____

7. Images of the usual mistakes and accidents that occur in a wedding are less popular.   _____

8. Photographers try to portray their clients as they want to look and not actually look.   _____

9. Brides often ask for nontraditional portraits but to buy traditional formal portraits.   _____

10. Photographers recommend a blend of casual and formal.   _____

11. Books that teach how to make wedding photographs often include hiding bald spots and double chins.   _____

12. The purpose of a ritual often is to teach the behaviors a culture values.   _____

13. Examine the neatly packaged, carefully scripted sequence of photographs in a wedding.   _____

14. What behaviors do they celebrate value?   _____

15. Think of them a method of preserving cultural continuity and community.   _____

PART 4 Style

UNIT 19

Sentence Unity and Consistency

Hodges': chapter 23
Writer's: chapter 23

In a unified sentence, ideas within the sentence are clearly related; excessive detail, mixed metaphors, and mixed constructions do not obscure the ideas; and subjects and predicates fit together logically.

Related ideas

Establish a clear relationship between the clauses in a sentence; develop unrelated ideas in separate sentences.

   When you write a compound sentence, you suggest that the two main clauses are closely related. Similarly, when you write a complex sentence, you make your reader expect a relationship between the ideas in the main and subordinate clauses.

Unclear	Noke only spoke Cambodian, and her parents enrolled her in a bilingual school.
Clear	Because Noke only spoke Cambodian, her parents enrolled her in a bilingual school.
Unclear	In school she heard for the first time her name pronounced in English, and nothing could have prepared her for that first day of school.
Clear	In school she heard for the first time her name pronounced in English. Nothing could have prepared her for that first day of school.

Arranging details

Avoid excessive or poorly ordered detail.

Unclear	When the county school board built the school, a few local politicians criticized it as being too nice. One benighted politician even said the school looked like the Taj Mahal and criticized the wide halls and large lockers and large foyer as wasteful and compared the eating area to a food court in a mall.
Clear	When the county school board built the school, a few local politicians criticized it as being too nice. They criticized the wasted space in the wide hallways, the large lockers, and the foyer. They compared the eating area to a food court in a mall. One benighted politician even said it looked like the Taj Mahal.

Mixed constructions

Be aware of mixed metaphors and mixed constructions.

Unclear	Lewis Andres who has led the fight for better schools in the county has been described as a grain of sand crying out in the wilderness.
Clear	Lewis Andres who has led the fight for better schools in the county has been described as a voice in the wilderness.
Unclear	When Andres pointed out that the new school actually cost less than previous schools angered some politicians.
Clear	When Andres pointed out that the new school actually cost less than previous schools, he angered some politicians. OR Andres' point that the new school actually cost less than previous schools angered some politicians.

Faulty predication

Make the subject and predicate of a sentence fit together grammatically and logically.

Illogical	The politicians' objections to the new school building are a serious controversy. [This sentence contains a mismatch between the plural subject, *objections,* and its singular complement, *controversy.* There is also a problem with logic: *objections* does not equal *controversy,* as the linking verb, *are,* suggests.]

Logical	The politicians' objections to the new school building have generated a serious controversy.
	[*Objections* can generate *controversy.*]
Illogical	The source of much of the controversy is because people disagree on how to spend tax dollars to support education.
	[*Source* does not equal *because*, as the linking verb *is*, suggests. A *because* clause serves as a modifier, not as a basic sentence part.]
Logical	Because people disagree on how to spend tax dollars to support education, the controversy arises.
	OR
	The source of the controversy is some people's disagreement on how to spend tax dollars to support education.
Illogical	In the emotional debate over money causes some citizens to lose sight of their real goal—improving education.
	[The writer has mistaken the object of a preposition, *debate*, for the subject of a sentence.]
Logical	The emotional debate over money causes some citizens to lose sight of their real goal—improving education.

Unnecessary shifts

As much as possible, maintain consistent grammatical structure, tone or style, and viewpoint.

As you read the following paragraph, notice how many times you must refocus your attention because of an unnecessary shift in number, tense, voice, or discourse.

All my life I have been around strong women. My grandmother became my nurse, my
tense
nanny, my companion, and my guide when I am two. One of my earliest memories is of
tense
her giving me a bath in front of the rumbling coal oil heater. It is cold, and I was
shivering despite the warm water, but her soft voice and gentle words make this a
pleasant memory. Even in these earliest memories I do not recall thinking of myself as
timid or unsure of myself. I was more a watcher, a careful observer who would think long
number
before they acted. Even today I carry those same traits to work every day. My grandmother
believed in the *Bible*; somewhere in the *Bible*, to her mind, lay the answer to every
tense **tense**
question. So she knew right from wrong and is quick to correct me if I stray. A typical
number **number**
child who deludes themselves into thinking they are wiser than an adult, I resisted her
voice
teachings. Today I am grieved when I think of the times that I disobeyed her.

tense

My mother is a somewhat more distant figure during my childhood. As I think
discourse   **person**   **person**
about her I wonder can I really capture her in words. We want to be accurate in our
person
representation of our parents, but my mother existed during my childhood at the

periphery of my life. I realize now, fortunately and early enough to tell her, that I

learned from her how to work—how to bend my shoulder to a task and persevere.

Define a word or an expression clearly and precisely.

The use of forms of the linking verb *be—is, are, was, can, be,* and so on—frequently
leads to faulty predication, particularly when the linking verb is followed by *when* or
where. By substituting a nonlinking verb such as *occur* or *is found,* you can often eliminate
the error in unity or logic.

Illogical	An example of the continuing debate is when the County Commission holds an open forum about funding schools.
Logical	The debate continues when the County Commission holds an open forum about funding schools.
	OR
	An example of the continuing debate is the County Commission's open forum on funding schools.

Avoid needless shifts in tense, mood, or voice.

Shift	During the discussion of school funding, the audience *listened* carefully but *said* nothing while the commissioners *speak* at length and loudly *argue* every point.
Consistent	During the discussion of school funding, the audience *listened* carefully but *said* nothing while the commissioners *spoke* at length and loudly *argued* every point.
Shift	One commissioner insists that he *be shown* as supporting the new school while his opponent *opposes* it.
	[shift from subjunctive mood to indicative mood]
Consistent	One commissioner insists that he *be shown* as supporting the new school while his opponent *be shown* as opposing it.
Shift	The commissioners created the forum to help the community; the best aspects of the community *are represented* by the forum.
Consistent	The commissioners created the forum to inform the community; the forum represents the best aspects of the community.

Be especially careful in writing essays on literature or historical topics to maintain a
consistent present tense while retelling a plot or an event.

Shift	In Horace's novel *The Second Coming* Molly *is characterized* as the matriarch of the family who *kept* them together during hard times.
	[shift from present tense to past tense]
Consistent	In Horace's novel *The Second Coming* Molly *is characterized* as the matriarch of the family who *keeps* them together during hard times.

Avoid needless shifts in person and in number.

Shift	When *we* read *The Second Coming, one* realizes that Molly is the moral center of the novel.
	[shift from first person to third person]
Consistent	When *we* read *The Second Coming we* realize that Molly is the moral center of the novel.
Shift	A *reader* who is unfamiliar with Horace's work will think that *they* are reading a contemporary version of Dickens.
	[shift in number]
Consistent	*Readers* who are unfamiliar with Horace's work will think that *they* are reading a contemporary version of Dickens.

Avoid needless shifts between indirect and direct discourse.

Shift	Although Horace has written for years, he still asks himself *if he is being true to his roots* and *would his grandmother approve.*
	[shift from declarative word order to interrogative word order]
Consistent	Although Horace has written for years, he still asks himself *if he is being true to his roots* and *if his grandmother would approve.*

OR

As he writes, Horace asks, "*Am I being true* to my roots? *Would my grandmother approve?*"

Avoid needless shifts in tone or style.

Shift	The older characters in Horace's fiction speak with a strong accent, are very mannered and courteous, and *interface with the church every Sunday.*
	[shift from formal style to computer jargon]
Consistent	. . . and attend church every Sunday.

Avoid needless shifts in perspective or viewpoint.

Shift
: Horace's study looks like a well-kept library; books festooned with improvised bookmarks and floppy disks storing every word that he has written indicate his packrat tendencies.

[shift from external perspective to internal perspective]

Consistent
: Horace's study looks like a well-kept library, but shelves of books festooned with improvised bookmarks and cartons of floppy disks storing every word that he has written indicate his packrat tendencies.

Unity in Sentence Structure

Name_____ Score _____

DIRECTIONS In the blanks, write *a, b, c, d,* or *e* to indicate whether the chief difficulty in each sentence is (a) an unclear relationship among ideas, (b) excessive detail and subordination, (c) mixed metaphors and mixed constructions, (d) an illogical combination of subject and predicate, or (e) unclear or imprecise definitions. Revise the sentences to make them effective.

EXAMPLE

Because Noke so eloquently explained her passion for education, ~~is why~~ she received the scholarship.   _____d_____

1. Noke's brother's climb up the ladder of success was nipped in the bud.   _____

2. Noke's philosophy believes in the liberating power of education.   _____

3. An example of Noke's determination to succeed is when she took extra hours of calculus to prepare herself for college.   _____

4. In Noke's early childhood, as her parents coped very well in America and worked steadily, and because they were optimistic and ambitious, they bought a house that was close to Noke's school.   _____

5. Her parents wanted Noke to walk to school, and their bright yellow house sat among the many white houses.   _____

6. When Noke's family moved into the neighborhood pleased their neighbors.   _____

7. An example of her family's popularity is when their neighbors helped them build a fence around their large garden.   _____

8. When the family had guests indicated their large circle of friends.   _____

9. The source of their popularity is because they are endlessly generous.   _____

10. Because they share the vegetables from their garden is one reason why they are so loved.   _____

11. Another example of their generosity is when they donated funds to build a local synagogue, although they are Buddhists.   _____

12. Noke was so eager to learn English that she mimicked her friends' speech, listened to them carefully, heard everything, and worked to understand every word they spoke.   _____

Shifts

Name_____ Score _____

DIRECTIONS Indicate the kind of shift in each of the following sentences by writing *a* (tense, mood, voice), *b* (person, number), *c* (discourse), or *d* (tone, style) in the blank. Then revise the sentence to eliminate the needless shift.

EXAMPLE

Lord Gavin's fiction ~~draws~~ *drew* heavily on his biography and was influenced by his early reading. ^   ___*a*___

1. Gavin's parents were raised on farms and come to live in town as young adults.   _____

2. Gavin's father worked with his three brothers to make a living on the farm, but he finally realizes that he must leave the farm.   _____

3. He asked himself can all of us live off this farm.   _____

4. A young man like his father is tied closely to the land, so when he left, it was heartbreaking.   _____

5. As one reads Gavin's first novel, we realize that Johnny is modeled closely after his father.   _____

6. Johnny comes to the small town of Jackson and went to work for a manufacturer of wheelbarrows.   _____

7. Here one works long hours, and he is paid low wages.   _____

8. In the rooming house where he lives he met a young woman, also on her own for the first time.   _____

9. After a night of passionate osculation, they realize that they are in love.   _____

10. They immediately wonder can they get married.   _____

11. His father adjusts only reluctantly to the move to town but became happier when he opened his own business.   _____

12. Marilyn, his mother, seems more adaptable and quickly worked herself into a better paying job.   _____

13. Then she also started her own business as a realtor.   _____

14. It is a job that required her to be good with people.   _____

15. Gavin's novel is now being made into a film, and he insists that his mother be played by Meryl Streep and that the actor to play his father is Nick Nolte.   _____

UNIT 20

Subordination and Coordination

Hodges': chapter 24
Writer's: chapters 24, 31

Good writers most often use subordination to extend their sentences and to vary the beginnings of sentences. (Subordinated additions to the sentence base are italicized in the following paragraph.)

> I am not going to offer you instructions on how to plant an herb garden, *one of those awful grids that demands basil be planted in the north quadrant and marjoram be planted in the east quadrant.*

As this example shows, grammatically subordinate structures may contain very important ideas.

The following sentence demonstrates coordination, which gives equal grammatical emphasis to two or more ideas.

> Instead, I will tell you how my herb garden has evolved, and I will share with you how I have come to value my herbs as a vital part of my life.

[Here, coordination gives equal emphasis to each of the two main clauses—*I will tell* and *I will share*. Notice also the coordination and equal emphasis achieved through the two noun clauses that serve as complements to the main verbs: *how my herb garden has evolved* and *how I have come.*]

Subordination and coordination

Instead of writing a series of short, choppy sentences, choose one idea for the sentence base, or main clause, and subordinate other ideas.

Because it stands apart from other sentences in a paragraph, a short sentence is often used for emphasis. But if the paragraph contains only short, choppy sentences, no single idea stands out, and the primary effect is monotony.

Short and Choppy	My garden plot includes a few vegetable plants. It also includes some herbs. And finally, it includes some edible flowers.
Subordination	My garden plot includes a few vegetable plants, some herbs, and some edible flowers.
	[The subordinated parts are complements.]
Short and Choppy	I placed a birdbath under a nearby tree. I hoped it would attract birds. The birds would also eat insects. That would keep the insects off my vegetables.
Subordination	I placed a birdbath under a nearby tree to attract birds who by eating insects would keep them off my vegetables.
	[The subordinated parts are an infinitive phrase and a clause.]

Instead of linking sentences primarily with coordinating conjunctions such as *and, so,* and *but* or with conjunctive adverbs such as *however* and *therefore,* extend most sentences through subordination.

Coordination of main clauses is helpful in developing a varied style because it gives equal emphasis to separate ideas.

The birds help to keep my plants healthy, and they add an attractive element of life to the garden.

But when ideas have a time, place, descriptive, or cause-and-consequence relationship, use subordination to show the connection between clauses while emphasizing the main idea.

Stringy	Cardinals are the first birds to the bath each morning, and they also get first chance at insects in the garden.
Related	Because cardinals are the first birds to the bath each morning, they also get first chance at insects in the garden.
	[shows cause and consequence]
Stringy	I needed to clean the birdbath, to pick the tomatoes, and to weed around the pepper plants before lunch, so I got up very early.
Related	I got up very early to clean the birdbath, to pick the tomatoes, and to weed around the pepper plants.
	[shows cause and consequence]

If you overdo or overlap subordination, your reader will have difficulty identifying the sentence base or main clause.

Unclear	The herbs that had been raised in a greenhouse and that were not mature and were not yet ready for transplanting

	should have been allowed to mature another few days. If they were more mature, they could better handle these spring nights that are unexpectedly cold.
Clear	Because the herbs came from a greenhouse, they were not yet ready to be transplanted and should have been allowed to mature another few days. More mature plants can better handle these unexpectedly cold spring nights.
Illogical	Because the students took the course from Chef Mario, they knew very little about cooking with herbs.
Logical	Because the students knew very little about cooking with herbs, they took the course from Chef Mario.

Punctuating dependent clauses and coordinated independent clauses

A comma usually follows an adverbial clause before an independent clause.

PATTERN   **Adverbial Clause,** Independent Clause.

Because it will rain all day, we will work inside the greenhouse.

Although I left the plant tray outside all night, the plants were not damaged.

When I complete this row, I will help Ryan with the watering.

A comma usually is unnecessary when the adverbial clause follows the independent clause.

The new plants were slightly damaged **when the storm hit last night.**

A comma precedes a coordinating conjunction that links two independent clauses.

	Conjunction	
Independent Clause,	and	Independent Clause.
Subject + Predicate,	but	Subject + Predicate.
	or	
	nor	
	for	
	so	
	yet	

We planted the herb bed, and then we took a break for lunch.

The school principal asked us to work another hour, but we had band practice.

The herbs are on the plant cart, or they are in the greenhouse.

Jaime won't help with the planting, nor will he eat herbs.

We asked him to dinner last night, for we planned to talk to him about participating more.

We want him to participate more, so he can go on field trips with us.

He wants to be with us, yet he will not discipline himself to do the work.

A semicolon may separate the independent clauses if one of the clauses contains commas.

I planted the marjoram along the border; and Lucy planted creeping thyme, scented geraniums, and ivy beneath the weeping cherry tree.

Subordination and Coordination
for Effectiveness

Name_____   Score _____

DIRECTIONS Combine each of the following groups of short, choppy sentences into one effective sentence. Express the most important idea in the main clause and put lesser ideas in subordinate clauses, phrases, or words. Use coordination when ideas should be given equal
emphasis.

EXAMPLE

Ansel Adams was born in 1902 and died in 1984. He was born of wealthy parents in San
Francisco. His first ambition was to be a classical musician.

*Ansel Adams (1902–1984) was born in San Francisco of wealthy parents
and first aspired to be a classical musician.*

1. In 1916 Adams made a trip to Yosemite Park. For the first time he experimented with
   photography. His first photographs were in the soft focus style of the time.

2. He pursued his musical career until 1930. By then he had been influenced by other
   photographers. The primary influence came from Paul Strand. Strand helped Adams
   develop a sharply focused style.

3. In 1937 he moved to Yosemite Park. Over the next decades he chronicled the beauty of
   Yosemite. Some of his most beautiful photographs feature familiar features of the park.
   They include the Merced River, Half Dome, and El Capitan.

4. Adams soon established himself as the greatest of America's nature photographers. He
   became the official photographer of the Sierra Club. He documented most of the great
   wilderness areas of the west.

5. Adams was not content to be only a nature photographer. He photographed architectural subjects. He also did some portraits. During World War II he also documented the conditions endured by interned Japanese Americans.

Subordination and Coordination
for Effectiveness

Name_____ **Score** _____

DIRECTIONS Rewrite each of the following stringy sentences to make one effective sentence. Express the most important idea in the main clause, and put lesser ideas in subordinate clauses, phrases, or words. Use coordination when ideas should be given equal emphasis.

EXAMPLE

Our teacher taught us how to make raised beds for the herbs, and he borrowed a truck so we could go to a plant nursery and buy railroad ties to make the beds; and while we were out, we bought soil and peat moss to put into the beds.

Our teacher borrowed a truck; took us to a plant nursery to buy railroad ties, soil, and peat moss; and taught us how to build raised beds in which to grow herbs.

1. Brad and Mateen loaded the ties, and they tied them down with ropes so the ties would not fall out during the drive.

2. Mateen does not like driving on the interstate, so he took surface streets, and that caused the trip to be much longer.

3. Charlene rode with Mateen, and she read the map to keep us going in the right direction, and being in charge is Charlene's favorite position.

4. Mateen's family tells stories of how easily he gets lost; they say he drives the same route to school each day; a new route would only get him lost.

5. Constructing the herb garden has been hard work, but it also has been a good project for the group, and we all will miss having it to share.

Subordination and Coordination
for Effectiveness

Name_____   **Score** _____

DIRECTIONS Rewrite the following paragraph, using subordination to eliminate the short, choppy sentences. Use coordination when ideas should be emphasized equally. (Not every sentence must be changed.) You will notice the improvements in style that proper subordination and coordination achieve if you read aloud first the original version of the paragraph and then your revision.

[1]I often watch visitors to our herb garden. [2]Many of them come here during their lunch breaks. [3]We have benches and tables. [4]They open sacks with their lunches and sit and talk. [5]They stroll among the beds. [6]Occasionally someone will kneel to look closely at a plant. [7]The signs ask people not to touch the plants. [8]Some of them cannot resist. [9]One woman always picks a tiny stem from the sweet woodruff. [10]A couple from across the street comes daily. [11]They pick a stem from the Italian parsley. [12]I should ask them to stop. [13]But I don't. [14]The garden is so inviting. [15]The plants are so edible. [16]It seems almost unnatural to pass by and not touch them. [17]Perhaps next year we should create a section explicitly for touching and picking. [18]We could plant highly aromatic herbs. [19]Rosemary and thyme and parsley would be good choices. [20]People could even put them on their lunches.

UNIT 21

Parallelism

Hodges': chapter 26
Writer's: chapter 25

Use parallel structure to give grammatically balanced treatment to items in a list or series and to parts of a compound construction.

Parallel structure means that a grammatical form is repeated—that an adjective is balanced by another adjective, a verb phrase by another verb phrase, a subordinate clause by another subordinate clause, and so on. Although ineffective repetition results in poor style, repetition to create parallel structure can result in very effective writing. The repetition of a sentence construction makes ideas clear to the reader, emphasizes those ideas, and provides coherence among the sentences in a paragraph.

Connectives such as *and, but,* and *or* often indicate that the writer intends to use parallel structure to balance the items in a list or series or the parts of a compound construction.

List or Series	We have read works by these three writers: a *collection* of stories by Zora Neale Hurston, one *volume* of Alice Walker's poetry, and Toni Morrison's *novel Beloved*.
Compound Parts	Elzie *has interviewed* Walker and *has ordered* taped interviews of Morrison and *has plans* to visit with two Hurston scholars.

Balancing similar grammatical elements

To achieve parallel structure, balance a verb with a verb, a prepositional phrase with a prepositional phrase, a subordinate clause with a subordinate clause, and so on.

The following examples are written in outline form to make the parallel structure, or lack of it, more noticeable. Correct parallel structure is indicated by vertical parallel lines, repeated words are printed in italics, and connectives are printed in boldface.

Awkward	Cheryl's committee recommends that she examine one writer in depth rather than examining three writers superficially.
Parallel	Cheryl's advisor recommends that she examine ‖ one writer in depth

	rather than || three writers superficially.

Awkward	As she researches Walker, all that she
	    reads in the journals,
	    learns from interviews,
	and
	    what her teachers tell her
	convinces her to concentrate on Sula.

Parallel	As she researches Walker, all that she || reads in the journals, || learns from taped interviews, **and** || hears from her teachers convinces her to concentrate on Sula.

Correlatives and parallel structure

To make the parallel clear, repeat a preposition, an article, the *to* of the infinitive, or the introductory word of a long phrase or clause. (Repeated elements of this type are printed in italics.)

Elzie's research has presented her
|| *with an opportunity to* travel
as well as
|| *with an opportunity to* meet Morrison.

However, she also has to spend her travel money wisely:
|| *to use it for* research
    || *of* Morrison
    or
    || *of* Walker
not
|| *to use it for* entertainment.

The committee believes
|| *that she will* conduct original research
and
|| *that she will* be a fine representative of the school.

In addition to coordinating conjunctions, correlatives like *both . . . and, either . . . or, neither . . . nor, not only . . . but also,* and *whether . . . or*—and expressions like *not* and *rather than* which introduce negative phrasing—are used to connect parallel structure. (These connectives are printed in boldface below.)

Elzie's trip to interview Walker is the result
    not only
|| of careful planning
    but also
|| of solid research.

Parallel Structure

Name_____ **Score** _____

DIRECTIONS Make an outline, like the outlines used in this section, of the parallel parts of the following sentences.

EXAMPLE

Victoria says that her interview with Mark McGwire on his charity work and that her interview with Sammy Sosa will focus on his new batting stance.

Victoria says
‖ that her interview with . . . work
and
‖ that her interview with . . . stance.

1. Three other students are also involved in research: Kim on Satchel Paige and Alice on Jackie Robinson and Morgan on Pete Rose.

2. Unfortunately the material on those three players is not concentrated in one library and is not easily accessed by computer.

3. The department has given Alice money to buy a modem, to have it installed, and to pay for an Internet connection.

4. Her earlier efforts to do research by computer have been fragmented and ineffective rather than focused and productive.

5. Our former head librarian was neither interested nor helpful.

6. Alice needs not only a modem but also a CD-ROM player.

7. With the CD-ROM player she will be able to access the *PMLA Bibliography,* to search the ERIC database, and to look up words in the *Oxford English Dictionary*.

Parallel Structure

Name _____ **Score** _____

DIRECTIONS Rewrite the following sentences to restore the parallel structure.

EXAMPLE

Our writing class is not so much a lecture but rather a workshop.

Our writing class is not so much a lecture as it is a workshop.

1. Every meeting is carefully planned, and it involves collaboration.

2. Some people in the class believe that the work produced by the small groups exceeds the work of a single student.

3. Class today is devoted to essay writing; it also is devoted to citation and to documentation.

4. Unlike previous classes, this class is not so much about writing but rather reading.

5. Some students think reading to each other seems more a luxury rather than a necessity.

6. Dr. White believes reading aloud will teach us two things: to recognize the voices of the writers and identifying key passages.

7. Unlike my other classes, this one forces me to be an active learner rather than passively watching.

8. Participation in the small groups was increased after the first two weeks and began to involve everyone.

9. We learned to rely on group judgement and relied on healthy disagreements.

10. Developed and named after our group leader, our group is called Sam's Group.

UNIT 22

Emphasis

Hodges': chapter 29
Writer's: chapter 26

Emphatic word order, used at the proper time, is an effective way to emphasize ideas and add variety to your writing. But emphatic sentence patterns should be saved for ideas that deserve special stress; if you use unusual patterns too often, your style will appear stilted.

Arrangement of words in a sentence

Gain emphasis by placing important words at the beginning or the end of a sentence—especially at the end—and unimportant words in the middle.

Unemphatic	San Francisco is the most beautiful city in America according to Ravi Meera.
Emphatic	San Francisco, according to Ravi Meera, is the most beautiful city in America.

Note: The beginning and the end (again, especially the end) are also the two most effective places to put important ideas in a paragraph or an essay.

A sentence that holds the reader in suspense until the end is called *periodic;* one that makes a complete statement and then adds detail is called *cumulative.* The cumulative sentence, which is more common, is usually easier to follow. But the periodic sentence, by reserving the main idea until the end, is more emphatic.

Cumulative	The city is the most romantic spot on the coast when it is enveloped by fog.
Periodic	When it is enveloped by fog, the city is the most romantic spot on the coast

Arrangement of ideas in ascending order

In a series, place ideas in order beginning with the least important one. Present the most important or most dramatic idea last.

Unemphatic	Ravi moved to San Francisco to work, to reinvent himself, and to study.
Emphatic	Ravi moved to San Francisco to work, to study, and to reinvent himself.

Active vs. passive voice

Unemphatic	The idea of moving was first mentioned in a letter to his parents.
Emphatic	He first mentioned the idea of moving to San Francisco in a letter to his parents.

Note: When the receiver of an action is more important than the doer, the passive voice will make the emphasis clear.

Ravi's application to the university was soon accepted.

Repetition of important words

The admissions counselor began the interview with a question about home, about Ravi's definition of home. Had his definition of home changed, she asked. Growing up in Idaho, Ravi said, home always had been a place. If someone asked him to name his home, he named the town near where his father had been born. So home was a fixed, unchanging, inherited place. Now that he had moved half way across the country he was seeking a new definition of home. Here he could shed the past and the fixed places and define home for himself—he could even define himself anew in this new home.

Caution: Repetition of a word produces only monotony unless the word is important enough to be emphasized.

Inversion of standard word order

Unemphatic	Large and various, the city attracted Ravi because it tempted him to dream.
Emphatic	The city, large and various, attracted Ravi because it tempted him to dream.
Unemphatic	Perhaps he could find a new life among its diverse people.
Emphatic	Perhaps, among its diverse people, he could find a new life.

Balanced sentence construction

Unemphatic	Perhaps Ravi's dreams will live in San Francisco, but Idaho would defeat them.
Emphatic	Perhaps Ravi's dreams will live in San Francisco; in Idaho they would not.

Emphasis

Name_____ **Score** _____

DIRECTIONS Rewrite each of the following sentences in emphatic word order.

EXAMPLE

There are many groups of performing artists in our community in addition to the modern dance group Stalking Cranes.

There are many groups of performing artists, including the modern dance group Stalking Cranes, in our community.

1. In the performing arts Jasmine felt out of place, but the dance group was different.

2. Perhaps she could free herself by learning to dance.

3. According to Jasmine a dancer succeeds by being disciplined, strong, and optimistic.

4. Jasmine reveals her talents in three dance pieces: the solo piece *Orion,* her best work; *Beaucoup,* a piece with two dancers; and *Lion de Paris,* another solo piece.

5. In 1999 *Orion* was given the Best Original Solo award at the Modern Dance Festival in Frankfort.

6. Jasmine has been recognized by critics as a particularly complete solo artist.

7. Confronting her need to prove herself as a dancer, Jasmine moved to New York.

8. Jasmine kept her dream alive but waitressed in a deli and sewed costumes at the Metropolitan Museum of Art.

9. Unforgettable images of Jasmine's courage and optimism appear in a recently released biography.

10. The attractive qualities of Jasmine may be caused by her thinking like an adventurer.

Emphasis

Name_____ **Score** _____

DIRECTIONS Write a paragraph in which you try to emphasize certain ideas by using three or more of the techniques explained in Unit 22. When you have finished, number the sentences in your paragraph and analyze what you have done to achieve emphasis by answering the questions on the next page.

SUGGESTED TOPICS

　　your favorite movie or story about sports

　　your definition of home

　　your experience with racial or cultural prejudice

　　why you would like to live in a different part of the country/world

PARAGRAPH

ANALYSIS

1. Did you use a short, abrupt sentence to emphasize an idea? If so, which sentence is
   used in this way? _____

   _____

2. Why did you emphasize this idea? _____

   _____

3. Which sentences in your paragraph have loose structure? _____

   _____

4. Which sentences have periodic structure? _____

5. Did you use any other techniques to achieve emphasis—for example, inverted word
   order, balanced structure, repetition of an important word or words? If so, list each
   technique used and the number of the sentence in which it appears.

   _____

   _____

   _____

   _____

   _____

   _____

   _____

UNIT 23

Variety

Hodges': chapters 29, 30
Writer's: chapter 27

Varying the length, structure, and beginning of sentences will make your style pleasing. On a few occasions, a series of short sentences that all begin with the subject is effective. In general, however, vary the length, structure, and beginnings of your sentences to achieve a fluid style.

Varying sentence length

Notice the effect in this passage of including sentences of various lengths.

Nurse Pat Eisberg drains the sink. She drops the newborn's old blanket and hat into an open hamper, peels a new blanket and hat from the pile on the right, and sticks the red baby on the right hand counter. She diapers him. She swaddles him: she folds the right corner of the blanket over him and rolls him back to tuck it under him; she brings up the bottom blanket corner over his chest; she wraps the left corner around and around, and his weight holds it tight as he lies on his back. Now he is tidy and compact, the size of a one-quart Thermos. She caps his conehead, and gives the bundle a push to slide it down the counter to the end of the line with the others she has just washed.

—Annie Dillard, *For the Time Being*

Making an important sentence noticeably shorter than the others will emphasize it.

My two men and I set out for the village where the man-eating tiger had made its last kill. We arrived just after midnight and were greeted by my old friend, Jin, who runs the local inn. He made us comfortable; and after we had settled in, he began to tell us of the tiger. It was a large male, he thought, that looked ill fed and gaunt. Perhaps, he said, it was sick or injured and began hunting people as a last resort. Thinking ahead to the next day, I asked where the tiger had taken its last victim. *There, he said, pointing to his porch.*

Varying sentence structure

Always following subject-first word order creates a monotonous style. Try these methods for varying that order.

Begin with an adverb or an adverbial phrase or clause.

Adverb	*Eventually,* they found a new doctor to take the case.
Adverbial Phrase	*In 1997,* her family moved to Sacramento.
Adverbial Clause	*After she married,* she decided to stay.

Begin with a prepositional phrase or a verbal phrase.

Prepositional Phrase	*In the interview,* she explained why she went to law school.
Verbal Phrase	*Studying the interview,* I can see connections between her father's career and hers.

Begin with a coordinating conjunction, a conjunctive adverb, or a transitional expression. However, be sure that the word or phrase shows the proper relation of one sentence to the sentence that precedes it.

Coordinating Conjunction	Because she wanted to attend a large university, she enrolled at U. C. Berkeley. *But* she sometimes wishes she had gone to a smaller, liberal arts school.
Conjunctive Adverb	*However,* she has decided to teach at a small school.
Transitional Expression	*Indeed,* Tatiana has even decided to forego private practice.

Begin with an appositive, an absolute phrase, or an introductory series.

Appositive	*An intellectually challenging experience,* her law and literature course teaches both legal issues and traditional fiction.
Absolute Phrase	*Their expressions intent,* the students leaned forward to better hear the discussion.
Introductory Series	*Idealistic, intelligent, passionate*—she is a wonderful role model.

Stringing simple sentences together to form compound sentences is less effective than experimenting with sentence structure. To revise an ineffective compound sentence, try one of these methods.

Make a compound sentence complex.

Compound	Tatiana emigrated from Russia, and she wanted more freedom and more economic opportunities.
Complex	Tatiana emigrated from Russia because she wanted more freedom and more economic opportunities.

Use a compound predicate in a simple sentence.

| Compound | Today immigrants arrive in America, and they have many of the same ambitions and fears of the earliest European settlers, and they are true pioneers. |
| Simple | Arriving in America today, immigrants have many of the same ambitions and fears of the earliest European settlers and are true pioneers. |

Use an appositive in a simple sentence.

| Compound | The American mythology is called "romanticism," and it refers to the ability to dream. |
| Simple | The American mythology, "romanticism," refers to the ability to dream. |

Use a prepositional or verbal phrase in a simple sentence.

| Compound | A dream is an expression of a desire for change, and it creates hope in us. |
| Simple | By expressing a desire for change, a dream creates hope in all of us. |

Occasionally separating the subject from the verb with words or phrases will vary the conventional subject-verb sequence. Each subject and verb in the following examples is italicized.

Subject-Verb	An immigrant's *home is* a place, but *it*, paradoxically, *is* a state of mind. [compound sentence]
Varied	An immigrant's *home*, a place, *is*, paradoxically, a state of mind. [simple sentence]
Subject-Verb	An *immigrant leaves* one home and *searches* for another.
Varied	An *immigrant*, having left one home, *searches* for another.

Varying kinds of sentences

Occasionally, use an interrogative, imperative, or exclamatory sentence instead of the more common declarative sentence.

We sat together on a ridge in Nepal, huddled under blankets, shivering, wet, and hungry. We were travelers, lost and wandering. A woman in a blue skirt walked across the road from her small house, lifting her skirt to avoid the mud. She held out her hands to us; in each palm lay a still warm boiled egg. "Where must you go now?" she asked.

[four declarative statements followed by a question]

—Cynthia Duke

Close your eyes. Remember. Recall the cold mist from the waterfall, the liquid song of the robin.   [three imperative sentences]

—Gwen White

Variety

Name_____ **Score** _____

DIRECTIONS Analyze the ways in which variety is achieved in the following paragraphs by answering the questions that follow.

[1]Calling yourself a Luddite is an old-fashioned way of admitting to technophobia. [2]Who remembers that Ned Ludd smashed stocking machines in the early nineteenth century? [3]I used to confess myself a Luddite, though, I who still do not own a word processor, perhaps believing still that I already have one: my head. [4]So I move through a series of electronic typewriters priced at about a hundred dollars. [5]Out of, or into, each I get three books, and then there is a shower of springs and bolts, indecent petulant buzzings, and the game is up. [6]I do not acquire a word processor because I hate screens, grays, compendious instructions; I like to see words line up in black on white, and I rather enjoy the fiddling handwork I have to do to make corrections, pasting the right version on to the old one, sometimes half a dozen lines at a time, at other times clipping a sliver of paper that bears one word only, then using a smear of Elmer's to fix it in place for all the world like a narcissistic philatelist. [7]Yet, these mundane and slimy operations done, I Xerox the page in question and slide it back where it belongs, usually destroying the palimpsest.

—Paul West, "The End of an Elite"

ANALYSIS

1. Which sentence is longest? _____

2. What is the purpose of the longest sentence? _____

_____

3. How many simple sentences are there? _____

   How many compound sentences? _____

   How many complex sentences? _____

4. What is the effect of phrasing sentence 2 as a question? _____

_____

5. Sentence 7 is a complex sentence. Identify the main clause and subordinate clause and

   the function of the modifiers. _____

_____

6. Which sentence begins with a transitional expression? _____

7. Which sentence uses a verbal as the subject? _____

8. How many of the sentences are declarative sentences? _____

Variety

Name_____ **Score** _____

DIRECTIONS Write a paragraph in which you use at least three of the methods for achieving variety explained in Unit 23. Because most people use varied sentence patterns when they write on subjects that they feel strongly about, traditional views that they can question, or topics that they can treat humorously, you may find one of the five beginnings suggested below useful. After you have finished your paragraphs, number your sentences and analyze what you have done to achieve variety by answering the questions on the next page.

SUGGESTED BEGINNINGS

1. I have witnessed a clash of genders while at work.

2. I have friends who are parents and students, and I admire them because . . .

3. If "home" is a state of mind, then I am most at home at . . . because . . .

4. Immigration laws should be more strongly enforced because . . .

5. My favorite woman character in a movie (or television series or book) is . . . because . . .

PARAGRAPH

ANALYSIS

1. Have you used a sentence or two that is noticeably shorter than the other sentences in the paragraph? _____

2. What type of sentence structure have you mainly used: simple, compound, or complex?
   _____

3. Which sentences have you begun with something other than the subject? _____
   _____

4. Does any sentence have a word or words inserted between the subject and verb or between the verb and complement? _____

5. Have you used any kind of sentence other than the declarative sentence?
   _____

PART 5 Writing

Learning to reason critically and logically and to judge the reasoning of other writers is an essential part of your preparation as a writer. In this section you will practice skills necessary for you to become an active and critical reader of your prose or of the prose of another writer.

Before you begin your first careful reading, take control of the reading experience by asking these questions:

How much time will I need to read this text carefully?

Do I already know anything about the subject that might help me understand the text?

Do I have strong feelings about the subject or author that might prevent my being objective as I read?

Do the title or section headings indicate anything about the ideas being developed or about the structure of the text?

If there is a table of contents, an index, or any kind of visual aids (pictures, graphs, drawings), what do they suggest?

What does the bibliography say about the research that the author has done?

What does a brief reading of the introduction and conclusion suggest about the middle sections of the text?

Should I read background material before reading this text?

Fact vs. opinion

Facts are pieces of information that can be verified through independent sources or procedures. Opinions are judgments that may or may not be based on facts.

Fact	The book was published in America.
Opinion	Paperback books are easier to read.

Facts, like opinions, can change. Curious and questioning readers are always prepared to examine facts with the same critical reading skills that they apply to opinions. They also are prepared to assimilate new ideas as the facts change.

As a critical reader you must expect writers to support their claims with appropriate evidence. You should expect evidence to be accurate, representative, sufficient, and verifiable.

As you read, evaluate the credibility of the writer according to these criteria:

Has the writer supported claims with evidence?

Has the writer revealed the sources of the evidence?

Has the writer acknowledged the legitimacy of other points of view?

Has the writer maintained an appropriate tone and style?

Has the writer reached a conclusion that the evidence will support?

Inductive vs. deductive reasoning

Every day at home the little girl spoke Spanish to members of her family. When she went to school, however, she struggled with the new language, English. Gradually she learned it too and easily slipped from one language into the other. But in her mind, Spanish was the family language, the language of private, intimate lives. English was the language for the rest of the world.

Inductive reasoning, as in the above example, is based on evidence: people observe or otherwise acquire facts—or what they believe to be facts—and they make a generalization based upon them. But, as the example of the girl thinking that everyone outside her family speaks English demonstrates, our reasoning sometimes fails us. When we reason inductively, we must take certain precautions: we must

- make sure the evidence is sufficient;
- make sure the conclusion fits the facts;
- make sure we do not ignore evidence; and
- make sure we do not present evidence that supports only our conclusion.

Critical thinkers understand deductive reasoning.

If you know that you have new Japanese neighbors and you hear a group of Asians across the street speaking a language that you do not recognize, you are likely to conclude that they are your new neighbors.

The kind of reasoning used in this example is based on a logical structure called a *syllogism.*

SYLLOGISM

Major Premise (usually a generalization): Female students are good at interpreting poems.

Minor Premise (a specific fact): Victoria is a female student.

Conclusion: Victoria is good at interpreting poems.

When the major premise and the minor premise are correctly related to form a conclusion, the syllogism is valid. Even if the reasoning is valid, however, the conclusion may be false if one of the premises is false. For instance, suppose that Victoria is not good at interpreting poems. That makes your major premise false; therefore, your conclusion is false. Based on the evidence that you had, your reasoning was valid, but your conclusion was false.

As you use deductive reasoning in your writing, particularly in argumentative papers, think very carefully about your premises to be sure your argument is sound—both true and valid. Also, consider your reader as you frame your premises: how difficult will it be for the reader to accept your premises?

Fallacies

Fallacies are faults in reasoning. They may result from misusing or misrepresenting evidence, from relying on faulty premises or omitting a needed premise, or from distorting the issues.

Non sequitur: A statement that does not follow logically from what has just been said—a conclusion that does not follow from the premises.

> Faulty   Of course Madeline Albright will speak at May Day exercises. Holly Hunter spoke last year, didn't she?
>
> [That Hunter spoke does not prove Albright will speak.]

Hasty generalization: A generalization based on too little evidence or on exceptional or biased evidence.

> Faulty   Two-year-olds are stubborn.
>
> [Undoubtedly, some two-year-olds are not stubborn.]

Ad hominem: Attacking the person who presents an issue rather than dealing logically with the issue itself.

> Faulty   She is unfit to serve on the city council because she has been married three times.
>
> [That she has been married three times does not invalidate her as a member of council.]

Bandwagon: An argument saying, in effect, "Everyone is doing or saying this, so you (or we) should too."

> Faulty   Everyone else is skipping class, so why shouldn't we?
>
> [That others do it does not make it right.]

Red herring: Dodging the real issue by drawing attention to an irrelevant issue.

> Faulty   Why worry about pollution of the river when we have homeless people on the streets?
>
> [Homeless people have nothing to do with pollution.]

False dilemma: Stating that only two alternatives exist when in fact there are more than two.

Faulty   We have only two choices: Immigrate to New Zealand or become inner-city teachers.

[Other possibilities exist.]

False analogy: The assumption that because two things are alike in some ways, they must be alike in other ways.

Faulty   Since the novels are both paperback and cost the same, one is probably as good as the other.

[The cost and paperback cover have nothing to do with quality.]

Equivocation: An assertion that falsely relies on the use of a term in two different senses.

Faulty   The teacher has the right to set the attendance policy, so she should do what is right and give unlimited cuts.

[The word *right* means both "a just claim" and "correct."]

Slippery slope: The assumption that one thing will lead to another as the first step in a downward spiral.

Faulty   The ethnic strife in Uganda shows that we are headed for another world war.

[The strife will not necessarily lead to such extreme results.]

Oversimplification: A statement that omits some important aspects of an issue.

Faulty   Now that you know how to use the computer, you can write the paper.

[Writing the paper is a far different activity from working the computer.]

Begging the question: An assertion that restates the point just made. Such an assertion is circular in that it draws as a conclusion a point stated in the premise.

Faulty   I did poorly on the test because I did not know the answers.

[Doing poorly and not knowing the answers are essentially the same thing.]

False cause: The mistake of assuming that because one event follows another, the first must be the cause of the second. (Also called *post hoc, ergo propter hoc,* or "after this, so because of this."

Faulty   Hurricane Sarah hit last summer and two months later the whole pecan grove died.

[The assumption is that the hurricane caused the death of the trees, an assumption that may not be true.]

Deduction

Name_____ Score _____

DIRECTIONS Prepare for a class discussion of the premises and conclusions in the following.

1. Major Premise: All angels are immaterial beings.

   Minor Premise: All immaterial beings are weightless.

   Conclusion: All angels are weightless.

2. Major Premise: One must choose between learning to use a computer and making costly errors.

   Minor Premise: John has learned to use a computer.

   Conclusion: Therefore, he will not make costly errors.

3. Major Premise: It is impossible to be both rich and unhappy.

   Minor Premise: Rucker is not rich.

   Conclusion: Therefore, he must be unhappy.

Fallacies

Name_____ Score _____

DIRECTIONS Identify the fallacies in the following sentences.

1. A volcano erupted in Japan last month; now pelicans are disappearing from the Gulf Coast.

   false cause _____

2. Sarah is so inexperienced because she has not done this before.

   _____

3. Why worry about the price of gasoline when the inner-city crime rate is so high?

   _____

4. The students are sick of hearing the administration's excuses about funding for the athletic team, but it is a sickness that we can cure by cutting the funds in half.

   _____

5. We have two choices: tear down the old gym or convert it into office space.

   _____

6. His questions to the visiting speaker were not well received because we all knew about his drug problem.

   _____

7. The Lyceum has only women speakers, and so does the honors program. It is time for us to do the same.

   _____

8. The singer is loud and tall; therefore, she will be good.

   _____

9. The classes are taught in the same building by teachers from the same department, so they should be identical classes.

   _____

10. Men just do not understand *haiku*.

   _____

UNIT 25

Paragraphs

Hodges': chapter 31
Writer's: chapter 2

We recognize the beginning of a new paragraph by the indention of the first word—about one inch when handwritten or five spaces when typewritten. A paragraph may range in length from 50 to 250 words, with an average length of about 100 words. The indention and length of a paragraph are signals to the reader that this unit of discourse will coherently and adequately develop an idea. As we read a paragraph, we expect to learn the controlling idea and to understand the relationship that each of the sentences has to that idea. And, finally, we expect the sentences to flow smoothly, so that we do not have to mentally fill in any words or phrases or stop reading at any point to refocus our attention.

Unity

Each sentence in a paragraph should be related to the central thought. In the following paragraph the controlling idea appears in italics. The words in boldface echo the controlling idea and help to unify the discussion.

1   *I want to be a modern woman.* I still have a nostalgic Afro, though it's **stylishly short.** I apologize to the hair industry, but frankly, I like both my kinks and my gray strands. Plus, being a sixties person, **glowing in the dark carries negative implications** for me. Most of my friends do wear **base, pancake, powder, eye make-up, lipstick, and always keep their nails in perfectly ovaled shapes with base, color, sealer, and oil for the cuticles.** Do I use these things? No. But neither do I put them down nor try to make my friends feel guilty for **not being natural.** There is something to be said **for improvement.** I've been known to comment: "Wow, you **look really good. Who does your nails?**" Why, I even have a dear friend who is a few months younger than I and uses **a night cream to guard against wrinkles.** Do I laugh? No, ma'am. I say, "Well, your **face is very, very, smooth,**" which (1) makes her feel good about her efforts and (2) keeps the friendship intact.
        —Nikki Giovanni, *Sacred Cows . . . And Other Edibles*

Giovanni explains in a humorous tone her aspiration to be a modern woman. Every sentence in the paragraph relates clearly and directly to the controlling idea. The reader never has to fill in gaps in the ideas or suffer the momentary confusion caused by a sentence that does not continue to develop the main idea.

A topic sentence embodies the central thought of a paragraph. Notice how the first sentence of paragraph 2 clearly signals the idea to be developed; obviously Woody Allen intends to define "spiffy."

2   Now, we all know when someone is dressed up, we say he looks "spiffy." The term owes its origin to Sir Oswald Spiffy, perhaps the most renowned fop of Victorian England. Heir to treacle millions, Spiffy squandered his money on clothes. It was said at one time he owned enough handkerchiefs for all the men, women, and children in Asia to blow their noses for seven years without stopping. Spiffy's sartorial innovations were legend, and he was the first man ever to wear gloves on his head. Because of extra-sensitive skin, Spiffy's underwear had to be made of the finest Nova Scotia salmon, carefully sliced by one particular tailor. His libertine attitudes involved him in several notorious scandals, and he eventually sued the government over the right to wear earmuffs while fondling a dwarf. In the end Spiffy died a broken man in Chichester, his total wardrobe reduced to kneepads and a sombrero.

—Woody Allen, *Without Feathers*

Often the main idea of a paragraph is stated at the beginning, as in paragraphs 1 and 2, but it may occur anywhere in the paragraph. In paragraph 3 the topic sentence is in the fourth sentence.

3   I was thinking one day about recent deaths of some of the traditional people and how difficult it is to maintain tradition. I was also thinking how important oral tradition is in helping maintain the values of culture, and how in a sense oral tradition is also an art form. As the elders pass on, the young people fill their places. Even though we know no one lives forever, no one dies if what they have gained by living is carried forward by those who follow—if we as individuals assume the responsibilities. This is easy to talk and write about, but it is hard to practice.

—Frank Lapeña, *News from Native California*

When a paragraph progresses from particulars to a generalization, the topic sentence is likely to occur at the end, as in paragraph 4.

4   So we have to remind ourselves that there are things that transcend generations, and the living force of that truth is carried by the person-to-person confidentiality of oral tradition. A lot depends upon the transmission of information from one person to another. Oral tradition is the educational tool of understanding the natural world.

—Frank Lapeña, *News from Native California*

A single topic sentence may serve for a sequence of two or more paragraphs. The first sentence in paragraph 5 unites paragraphs 5 and 6.

5   We found the Americans as strange in their customs as they probably found us. Immediately we discovered that there were no *mercados* and that when shopping you

did not put the groceries in a *chiquihuite*. Instead everything was in cans or in card-board boxes or each item was put in a brown paper bag. There were neighborhood grocery stores at the corners and some big ones uptown, but no *mercado*. The gro-cers did not give children a *pilón*, they did not stand at the door and coax you to come in and buy, as they did in Mazatlán. The fruits and vegetables were displayed on counters instead of being piled up on the floor. The stores smelled of fly spray and oiled floors, not of fresh pineapple and limes.

6 Neither was there a plaza, only parks which had no bandstands, no concerts every Thursday, no Judases exploding on Holy Week, and no promenades of boys going one way and the girls the other. There were no parks in the *barrio;* and the ones uptown were cold and rainy in winter, and in summer there was no place to sit except on the grass. When there were celebrations nobody set off rockets in the parks, much less on the street in front of your house to announce to the neighbor-hood that a wedding or a baptism was taking place. Sacramento did not have a *mer-cado* and a plaza with the cathedral to one side and the Palacio de Gobierno on another to make it obvious that there and nowhere else was the center of the town.

—Ernesto Galarza, *Barrio Boy*

Occasionally no topic sentence is necessary because the details clearly imply the con-trolling idea.

7 We were working at the laundry when a delivery boy came from the Rexall drug-store around the corner. He had a pale blue box of pills, but nobody was sick. Reading the label we saw that it belonged to another Chinese family, Crazy Mary's family. "Not ours," said my father. He pointed out the name to the delivery ghost, [Kingston uses "ghost" to designate a non-Chinese person.] who took the pills back. My mother muttered for an hour, and then her anger boiled over. "That ghost! That dead ghost! How dare he come to the wrong house?" She could not concentrate on her marking and pressing. "A mistake! Huh!" I was getting angry myself. She fumed. She made our press crash and hiss. "Revenge. We've got to avenge this wrong on our future, our health, and on our lives. Nobody's going to sicken my children and get away with it." We brothers and sisters did not look at one another. She would do something awful, something embarrassing. She'd already been hinting that during the next eclipse we slam pot lids together to scare the frog from swallowing the moon. (The word for "eclipse" is *frog-swallowing-the-moon*.) When we had not banged lids at the last eclipse and the shadow kept receding anyway, she'd said, "The villagers must be banging and clanging very loudly back home in China."

—Maxine Hong Kingston, *Woman Warrior*

Coherence and transitions

The following paragraphs illustrate several ways to illustrate ideas clearly and logically in a paragraph. The choice depends on the context of the writing and on the writer's purpose.

Time order

8   There is a story about the way the first pipe came to us. A very long time ago, they say, two scouts were out looking for bison; and when they came to the top of a high hill and looked north, they saw something coming a long way off, and when it came close they cried out, "It is a woman!," and it was. Then one of the scouts, being foolish, had bad thoughts and spoke them; but the other said: "That is a sacred woman; throw all bad thoughts away." When she came still closer, they saw that she wore a fine white buckskin dress, that her hair was very long and that she was young and very beautiful. And she knew their thoughts and said in a voice that was like singing: "You do not know me, but if you want to do as you think, you may come." And the foolish one went; but just as he stood before her, there was a white cloud that came and covered them. And the beautiful young woman came out of the cloud, and when it blew away the foolish man was a skeleton covered with worms.

—Black Elk, *Black Elk Speaks*

Paragraph 9 demonstrates space order, an arrangement that is particularly useful for descriptions.

Space order

9   The kitchen was dominated by a large Victorian china closet, and the built-in wall shelves were lined with oilcloth, trimmed with ruffle, both decorated by brilliant and miniature fruits. Prominent on a wall of the kitchen was a large reproduction of a still life, a harvest table full of produce, framed and under glass. From it, I learned to identify apples, pumpkins, bananas, pears, grapes, and melons, and "peaches without worms." A joke between my mother and me. (A peach we had bought in the city market, under the New Haven's elevated tracks, bore, like the trains above, passengers.)

—Jack Agueros, *The Immigrant Experience:*
The Anguish of Becoming American

Order of importance

10   The ethnic American is overtaxed and underserved at every level of government. First, he cannot afford fancy lawyers or expensive lobbyists getting him tax breaks on his income. Yet, being a homeowner he shoulders the burden of property taxes which are the primary revenue producers for the municipalities where he lives. Second, he knows that one major illness in his family can wipe him out financially. If he needs a nursing home for an elderly family member, he is not eligible for financial assistance—he earns too much. And last and most important to him, his children attend parochial schools which receive little government assistance. Thus his future, his children, are imperiled.

—Guillermo Gómez-Peña, "Documented/Undocumented"

Sometimes the movement within the paragraphs is from general to specific or from specific to general—as paragraphs 11 and 12 demonstrate.

General to specific; specific to general

11   Today, eight years after my departure (from Mexico), when they ask me for my nationality or ethnic identity, I can't respond with one word, since my "identity" now possesses multiple repertoires: I am Mexican, but I am also Chicano and Latin American. At the border they call me *chilango* or *mexiquillo;* in Mexico City it's *pocho* or *norteno;* and in Europe it's *sudaca.* The Anglos call me "Hispanic" or "Latino," and the Germans have, on more than one occasion, confused me with Turks or Italians. My wife Emilia is Anglo-Italian, but speaks Spanish with an Argentine accent, and together we walk amid the rubble of the Tower of Babble of our American post-modernity.

—Guillermo Gómez-Peña, "Documented/Undocumented"

12   Discrimination means discernment; it means the ability to perceive the truth, to use good judgment and to profit accordingly. *The Oxford English Dictionary* traces this understanding of the word back to 1648 and demonstrates that for the next 300 years, "discrimination" was a virtue, not a vice. Thus, when a character in a nine-teenth-century novel makes a happy marriage, Dickens has another character remark, "It does credit to your discrimination that you should have found such a very excel-lent young woman."

—Robert Keith Miller, "Discrimination Is a Virtue"

One common form of the general-to-specific pattern is topic-restriction-illustration. The writer announces the topic, restricts or qualifies it, and then illustrates it.

Topic-restriction-illustration

13   America is not a melting pot. It is a sizzling cauldron for the ethnic American who feels that he has been politically extorted by both government and private enterprise. The ethnic American is sick of being stereotyped as a racist and dullard by phony white liberals, pseudo black militants and patronizing bureaucrats. He pays the bill for every major government program and gets nothing or little in the way of return. Tricked by the political rhetoric of the illusionary funding for black-oriented social programs, he turns his anger to race—when he himself is the victim of class preju-dice. He has worked hard all of his life to become a "good American"; he and his sons have fought on every battlefield" then he is made fun of because he likes the flag.

—Barbara Mikulski, *Poles in the Americas: 1608–1972*

In the problem-solution pattern, the first sentence states a problem and the solution follows.

Problem-solution

14   Unity is not automatically bequeathed to people of color. Racism translates the differences among us into *relatively* preferential treatment for some at the expense of others, promoting internalized racism and cross-racial hostility. Disunity among peo-ple of color due to the exploitation of differences is an inherent part of the system of racism. The potential for unity is there and the power is tremendous—witness the recent Civil Rights Movement. For unity to develop and continue to exist, the distrust and discord ever-present among us must be replaced.

—Virginia R. Harris and Trinity A. Ordoña,
Hacienda Caras: Making Face, Making Soul

In the question-answer pattern, the topic sentence asks a question and the supporting sentences answer it.

Question-answer

15   Where will the American Indian homeless go to avoid freezing to death this winter? Yes, that's right; it's hard for some people to believe, but it's true. There are a lot of American Indians who are homeless; as a matter of fact, 1 out of 18 homeless on skidrow is Indian.

—Gary Tewalestewa, "American Indians: Homeless
in Their Own Homeland"

Many types of development exist, and you will have occasion to create types that combine or modify those represented in the preceding paragraphs. Remember, however, that your goal as a writer is to make your sequence of thought clear.

Transitional devices such as pronouns, repetition of key words or ideas, appropriate conjunctions and other transitional expressions, and parallel structures help create a coherent paragraph. Paragraph 16 exhibits several transitional devices (in boldface).

16   In individual interviews **we asked** each **woman** what **she thought** would stay with her about her experiences in the school or program she attended. **We asked her** to tell us about specific academic and nonacademic experiences, about **good and bad** teachers, **good and bad** assignments, **good and bad** programs or courses. **We asked her** whether **she thought** that **her** participation in the program had changed the way **she though**t about herself or the world. **We asked:** "In your learning here, have **you** come across an idea that made **you** see things differently?" "What has been most helpful to **you** about this place?" "Are there things it doesn't provide that are important to **you?** Things **you** would like to learn that **you** can't learn here?" **Finally, we asked,** "Looking back over **your** whole life, can **you tell us** about a really powerful learning experience that **you've had,** in or out of school?"

—Blythe McVicker Clinchy, et al., "Connected Education for Women"

In this finely crafted paragraph the authors use several devices to achieve coherence.

Pronoun reference: Repetition of *we, her, she,* and *you.*

Repetition of key words or ideas: The repeated *we asked* and *she thought.*

Parallel structure: The structure depends on repeated questions put to women students by women questioners. The repeated questions and pronouns make the paragraph strongly coherent.

The authors could have used conjunctions and other transitional expressions to link sentences, but they did not need them—except for *finally* near the end which helps provide closure.

You may find the following list of connectives useful.

Alternative and Addition	or, nor, and, then, moreover, further, furthermore, besides, likewise, also, too, again, in addition, even more important, next, first, second, third, in the first place, in the second place, finally, last
Comparison	similarly, likewise, in like manner
Contrast	but, yet, or, and yet, however, still, nevertheless, on the other hand, on the contrary, conversely, even so, notwithstanding, for all that, in contrast, at the same time, although this may be true, otherwise, nonetheless
Place	here, beyond, nearby, opposite to, adjacent to, on the opposite side
Purpose	to this end, for this purpose, with this object
Cause, Result	so, for, hence, therefore, accordingly, consequently, thus, thereupon, as a result, then
Summary, Repetition, Exemplification, Intensification	to sum up, in brief, on the whole, in sum, in short, as I have said, in other words, that is, to be sure, as has been noted, for example, for instance, in fact, indeed, to tell the truth, in any event
Time	meanwhile, at length, soon, after a few days, in the meantime, afterward, later, now then, in the past

Clear writing demands clear transitions between paragraphs as well as between sentences. Notice the transitional devices used in the following paragraphs in which Allene Guss Grognet discusses second-language learning among older immigrants.

17   Taking adult learning theory, or andragogy, seriously can help build successes. Andragogy assumes that learning situations take into account the experiences of the learner, providing the opportunity for new learning to be related to previous experiences. Furthermore, the adult learner should be involved in analyzing both the new and the old experiences.

Andragogy also assumes that for the adult, readiness to learn is decreasingly the product of biological development or academic pressure, and increasingly the product of the desire to accomplish tasks required in work and/or social roles.

Finally, andragogy assumes that children have more of a subject-centered orientation to learning, whereas adults tend to have a problem-solving orientation to learning (e.g., The child wants to learn "arithmetic," while the adult may want to learn to add and subtract in order to keep a check book.). This means that language learning must incorporate strategies appropriate to adult learners. Learning situations which adults perceive as putting them in the position of being treated as children are bound to interfere with their learning.

—Allene Guss Grognet, "Elderly Refugees and Language Learning"

The transitional expressions—*furthermore, also, finally*—effectively signal the relationships between ideas; the content of the paragraphs bears out the signal. Other similarly useful expressions are

First . . . then . . . next . . . finally . . .

Then . . . Now . . . Soon . . . Later . . .

One . . . Another . . . Still another . . .

Some . . . Others . . . Still others . . .

A few . . . Many . . . More . . . Most . . .

Just as significant . . . More important . . . Most important of all . . .

Details and examples

Sometimes very brief paragraphs, even paragraphs of one sentence, are appropriate. But most very brief paragraphs are brief because their topics are not developed or because they are not paragraphs at all—they are fragments of paragraphs which actually belong elsewhere in the writing. Analyze the following paragraphs to decide how they are inadequately developed and what revision would improve them.

18   Now that I can have her only in memory, I see my grandmother in the several postures that were peculiar to her: standing at the wood stove on a winter morning and turning meat in a great iron skillet; sitting at the south window, bent above her beadwork, and afterwards, when her vision failed, looking down for a long time into the fold of her hands; going out upon a cane, very slowly as she did when the weight of age came upon her; praying.

19   I remember her most often at prayer. She made long, rambling prayers out of suffering and hope, having seen many things. I was never sure that I had the right to hear, so exclusive were they of all mere custom and company. The last time I saw her she prayed standing by the side of her bed at night stark naked to the waist, the light of a kerosene lamp moving upon her dark skin. Her long, black hair, always drawn and braided in the day, lay upon her shoulders and against her breasts like a shawl.

20   I do not speak Kiowa, and I never understood her prayers, but there was something inherently sad in the sound, some merest hesitation upon the syllables of sorrow. She began in a high and descending pitch, exhausting her breath to silence; then again and again—and always the same intensity of effort, of something that is, and is not like urgency in the human voice. Transported so in the dancing light among the shadows of her room, she seemed beyond the reach of time. But that was illusion; I think I knew then that I should not see her again.

—N. Scott Momaday, *The Way to Rainy Mountain*

These three paragraphs are paragraphs only insofar as indention denotes a paragraph. Together, however, they form a complete discussion of the idea stated in the first sentence.

You always need to know the details that support the idea you are writing about. Occasionally you may not use those details, but knowing them will make it possible for you to write about the idea with confidence.

In the following paragraph, the author explains some of the logic of Black English.

21   Black English also differs considerably from Standard English in the various ways in which negative statements are structured. The Black English *He ain't go* is not simply the equivalent of the standard *He didn't go*. The speaker of Black English is not using *ain't* as a past tense, but rather to express the negative for the momentary act of going, whether it happened in the past or is happening right now. If the Black English speaker, on the other hand, wants to speak of someone who is habitually the kind of person who does not go, he would say, *He ain't goin*. *Ain't* also serves several other functions in Black English. *Dey ain't like dat* might be thought by speakers of Standard to mean *"They aren't like that"*—but it actually means *"They didn't like that,"* because in this usage *ain't* is the negative of the auxiliary verb *to do*. *Ain't* can also emphasize a negation by doubling it, as in *He ain't no rich*. And in what would be a negative *if*-clause in Standard English, the rules of Black English eliminate the *if* and invert the verb—with the result that the equivalent of the Standard *He doesn't know if she can go* is the Black English *He don't know can she go*.

—Peter Farb, *Word Play: What Happens When People Talk*

The first sentence suggests the purpose for the details—to illustrate Farb's contention that Black English structures negative statements differently than Standard English. With that in the reader's mind, the details build a picture of a complex linguistic system.

Several closely related examples or one striking example can illustrate a generalization, as in this paragraph about poverty.

22   Poverty is asking for help. Have you ever had to ask for help, knowing your children will suffer unless you get it? Think about asking for a loan from a relative, if this is the only way you can imagine asking for help. I will tell you how it feels. You find out where the office is that you are supposed to visit. You circle the block four or five times. Thinking of your children, you go tell her that you need help. That never is the person that you need to see. You go see another person, and after spilling the whole shame of poverty all over the desk between you, you find that this isn't the right office after all—you must repeat the whole process, and it never is any easier at the next place.

—Jo Goodwin Parker, "What Good Is Poverty?"

Paragraphs

Name _____ **Score** _____

DIRECTIONS Discuss the unity, coherence, and development of the following paragraphs by answering the questions that follow them.

PARAGRAPH ONE

[1]Yunna Paiyao is used for all sorts of hemorrhage. [2]It can be sprinkled right on a bleeding wound. [3]The European equivalent is yarrow. [4]When I have cut myself and the bleeding wouldn't stop I have gone in the yard and grabbed a feathery sprig of yarrow (*Millefolium,* so called for the thousands of little divisions of the leaf), chewed it into a wad, and stuck it in the wound. [5]Both the bleeding and pain stopped almost instantly. [6]Homeopaths use a tincture of *Millefolium* to quell all kinds of hemorrhages, from nosebleed to bleeding bowels or hemorrhoids. [7]Plantain leaves, another common lawn weed, are also useful for cuts. [8]When my daughter had a laceration that gaped, she decided to experiment by covering it with lightly crushed plantain leaf rather than having stitches. [9]We bandaged it and waited two days—almost afraid to unveil the results. [10]What we found then was a line so fine that it was barely visible. [11]I can't say there was no discomfort, however. [12]She had complained that it seemed "too tight"—as though it were drawing shut.

—Rudolph Ballentine, M.D., *Radical Healing*

QUESTIONS

1. Which sentence states the controlling idea? _____

2. What are the keys words in the controlling idea? _____

_____

_____

3. What devices help achieve unity? _____

_____

_____

4. How does the writer develop the controlling idea? _____

_____

_____

PARAGRAPH TWO

[1]Yet of all the blooms in a Muslim garden, the tulip was regarded as the holiest, and the Turkish passion for this flower went far beyond mere appreciation of its beauty. [2]For the Ottomans as for the Persians, it had a tremendous symbolic importance and was literally regarded as the flower of God because, in Arabic script, the letters that make up *lale,* the Turkish word for tulip, are the same as those that form *Allah.* [3]The tulip also

represented the virtue of modesty before God: [4]When in full bloom, it bows its head. [5]After the proscription on images of living things was finally relaxed, in the course of the fifteenth and early sixteenth centuries, tulips were often depicted in Ottoman illustrations of the Garden of Eden, blossoming beneath the fruit trees where Eve was tempted. [6]Turks who willingly gave their lives in battle, believing that death in service of Islam was the surest passport to a paradise of meadowlands where divinely beautiful houris would serve them the wine they were denied on earth, fully expected to find their heaven strewn with tulips. [7]To an Ottoman gardener, therefore, it was one of the handful of flowers of the first value, and only the rose, the narcissus, the carnation, and the hyacinth were worthy to be classed alongside it. [8]All other blooms, however rare, however beautiful, were considered "wildflowers" and were cultivated only occasionally. [9]For this reason it is not hard to believe that tulips accompanied the Turks as they swept westward from Asia into Europe.

—Mike Dash, *Tulipo Mania*

QUESTIONS

1. Which sentence states the controlling idea? _____

2. What transitional devices are used in sentences 3 and 7? _____

   _____

   _____

3. What type of order is used? _____

4. What is the main method used to develop the controlling idea? _____

   _____

   _____

UNIT 26

The Essay

Hodges': chapter 32
Writer's: chapters 1, 2, 3

The principles that you studied for writing effective paragraphs—unity, coherence, and adequate development—are equally important for writing a whole composition. But even more than for a paragraph, the writing of an essay requires a complex of activities—planning, drafting, and revising—that is seldom linear or neat. Usually composing will require you to engage in the three activities several times as you discover, develop, and create the final form of a composition. Whatever repetition or messiness you experience, you must learn to be patient with yourself at the same time you work to improve. The more aware you become of the conventions of writing and of what works well for you, the better and easier your writing will become.

Purpose, audience, and occasion

Although it is sometimes difficult to identify, writing always has a purpose. Once you know what a given composition is supposed to accomplish, the composing process will begin to proceed smoothly.

The purposes of nonfiction writing may be classified as *expressive, informative,* and *persuasive.* Very seldom will you write an extended composition that has only one of these purposes, but the terms will help you describe what you wish to write or analyze what you have written.

Expressive writing emphasizes a writer's feelings and reactions to the world. If you keep a diary or journal or write personal letters in which you recount your responses to your experience, you are engaging in expressive writing.

Informative writing focuses a reader's attention on the objective world, not on the writer's responses to that world. This textbook is a good example of informative writing as it leads you to think about the ideas and actions that help you learn to write. News articles, encyclopedia articles, science reports, and other technical writing that transmits information to a specific audience—all are good examples of informative writing.

Persuasive writing attempts to affect a reader's opinions and/or actions. It relies specifically on evidence and logical reasoning. And as you attempt to persuade, you are likely to employ expressive and informative writing.

Whatever final purpose you decide on, you must have a clear picture in your mind of what you intend to accomplish. Only then can you begin to control your writing.

In recent years many authors have written books that make challenging subjects available to the general public—Richard Selzer's *Confessions of a Knife* and Stephen Jay Gould's *Wonderful Life* come to mind. Selzer and Gould are highly trained scientists who can write very specialized articles and books for equally specialized audiences. Both writers are comfortable with the jargon or technical language that is appropriate to their specialized audiences. Fortunately for us, however, they are also comfortable writing for readers who understand little about such technical training and subjects. When they write to us—a general audience—they simply assume that we are curious, interested, attentive readers. They either omit the jargon or translate it into diction we can understand; they explain ideas in terms that we know.

Selzer and Gould are particularly good at infusing dry, technical information with a human element. Selzer describes a parasite that has entered the human body in terms that make it seem supernatural, perhaps even demonic. Gould manages to incorporate technical language into his prose, and to define it, so that we can understand what he says. He describes a worm known to us only through fossils. It is named Pikaia and is "an attractive species, a laterally compressed ribbon-shaped creature some two inches in length." Furthermore, "It is a chordate, a member of our own phylum . . . with a notochord, the stiffened dorsal rod that gives our phylum, Chordata, its name."

Selzer and Gould succeed as writers—in large part—because they know their audiences. They bring us information in a language that we find both vivid and accessible; as a result, we as general readers get to see and know what they see and know.

Each writing assignment presents its own context, its own time, place, and climate. If your instructor weights the grading of your essays during the semester, your last essay may count double the grade of an earlier essay; that weighting is one factor that alters the occasion of your writing. If you write an essay as part of a timed exam in a controlled setting, the time, place, and climate of that restricted circumstance will affect your writing; and you must be aware of the occasion so that you can address the unique demands it places on you as a writer.

For many writing assignments occasion is less important, or at least apparently so. However, you will exercise more control over your developing ability to write if you keep in mind the occasion as a determining factor.

Finding an appropriate topic

In college writing, an "appropriate subject" is one that meets the needs of the writing assignment. Sometimes your writing instructor assigns a topic, in which case you can immediately begin considering the needs of the audience, what aspects of the topic you want to emphasize, and how the composition, should be organized. Many times, however, you will be allowed to choose a topic; for some students, this freedom feels more like an obstacle to successful writing than an opportunity. In this case, your personal experience, knowledge, and interests are a good place to start looking for subject matter. You can write an interesting, stimulating paper on almost anything you care about.

Sometimes you will need to choose a topic outside your experience. For example, a history professor who asks you to write a composition on some aspect of nineteenth-century Russia will want you to demonstrate your command of certain information rather than your personal experience or feelings. But, again, you can write a better paper if you find an aspect of the topic that interests you.

And, of course, two other vital practical considerations are time and length. If you have to write a paper in a few hours, choose a subject you already know about—not one that requires research. If you have to write a paper of 500 to 600 words on Kate Chopin, do not choose "Kate Chopin's Writing Career" as your subject. Choose "Chopin's Fiction and Victorian Morals" or "Chopin's Views on Marriage." Find a subject appropriate to the amount of time you have and the length the instructor has asked for.

Focusing on a topic

Once you have a general subject in mind, the following methods, used singly or in combination, will help you explore it.

Write down everything that comes to mind. Disregard grammar, spelling, and diction—just write. Here is a typical list one student made as she thought about a very broad subject: Home.

Michigan

Ann Arbor

parents and siblings

my cats

homesickness

friends

what I miss when I am away

where they have to take me when I return

how to make a home

is it a place

is it also something in my mind

what do I want from a home

it gives me security and comfort—any place could do that

it lets me be me

it is where I am free to be me

I carry home with me—this is it

The list demonstrates the student's discovery of a possible subject—the idea that being at home is the same as feeling the freedom to be yourself and that you carry home with you.

Journalists typically ask *who? what? when? where? how?* and *why?* Answering those questions about a topic may help you find your subject. Look at the preceding list and consider the benefit of asking these questions about *home.* Simply asking why you need a home will stimulate ideas.

Think about the subject home from three approaches—*static, dynamic,* and *relative.* A *static* approach focuses on what a home is or on an example of a home. A *dynamic* perspective focuses on action and change: How does a home affect us? How do we create a home? Can a home change? A *relative* perspective examines relationships within a system. Think about the connection between home and family. Or between home and our sense of identity.

The development strategies discussed earlier suggest ways of thinking about a topic. For example,

Narration: What is a story that focuses on home?

Process: How can you create a home?

Cause and Consequence: How does home change you?

Description: What does home look like?

Definition: What is home?

Classification and Division: What does one lose by not having a home?

Example: What are some benefits?

Comparison and Contrast: How is a home different from a house? Where is an immigrant's home?

During the previous discussions of exploring the subject, we also have examined limiting and finally focusing the subject—getting a clear idea of what you want to accomplish for a certain audience in a paper of a certain length. Suppose, for example, we move from the very broad topic, home, to topics that are more limited.

home ⟶ place ⟶ state of mind ⟶ people who seem at home anywhere ⟶ immigrants ⟶ the psychology of creating a new home

The last topic—What must immigrants do psychologically to create a new home?—focuses the subject. You now know the limits of your discussion, and you know what kind of information you must research.

Establishing a thesis

We earlier suggested a variety of ways to limit and focus a subject. We finally narrowed the broad subject, home, into a single specific question: What must immigrants do psychologically to create a new home? The question demonstrates a limited, focused subject. The paper we write will answer the question for ourselves and our reader. At some point in the composing process we need to condense that answer into a single statement that clearly suggests the thesis of the composition—the idea that binds together the discussion. For example,

Vague Thesis	It is difficult for immigrants to feel at home.
Improved Thesis	An immigrant must embrace the future, and to some extent reject the past, if he is to construct a new home.

The vague thesis statement is as true as the improved one, but it helps neither the writer nor the reader. The word "difficult" expresses no clear focus for the writer; therefore, the reader is not sure what to expect. The improved thesis statement focuses by explaining "difficult": an immigrant must reject the past if he is to embrace the future.

The thesis statement helps a writer decide how to construct the essay. For example, a series of brief case studies of immigrants could illustrate the two halves of the thesis: (1) rejecting the past and (2) embracing the future. And, of course, a reader will interpret a thesis statement as an indication of the form and content of the discussion.

Depending on the method of development, the thesis statement may occur anywhere in the essay. Or it may not need to be stated at all. For the reader's benefit, however, the thesis statement usually appears at or near the beginning of the essay. At other points in the discussion the writer may repeat the thesis entirely—although in different terms—or in part. The repetition helps to guide the writing and reading process.

Arranging ideas

The strategies for developing paragraphs and possible essay topics also work very well for developing longer pieces of writing. *Exemplification, narration, process, cause and consequence, classification, definition, description, analysis,* and *comparison and contrast*—one of these or a combination of them can be used for organizing your paper effectively.

Eventually every writer develops a working plan; if you intend to write successfully, you must find one that works well for you and master it. Some writers use a very informal plan; perhaps a list is sufficient for them. They jot down ideas, cross out some, move others to another location in the list, draw lines to suggest connections or overlap. They are comfortable with this relatively imprecise kind of plan, knowing that they will write, revise, write some more, and finally clarify what to say and how to say it. The plan remains extremely flexible.

An informal plan may begin with a list and evolve into an informal outline. The earlier list about home could evolve into this informal outline.

Informal outline

Thesis statement: An immigrant must embrace the future and, to some extent, reject the past if he is to create a new home.

1. Why the Shin family left Korea
2. Gina's description of arriving in America
3. The Shin family business and the freedom it gives them
4. The Chan family leaves Thailand
5. Why they chose to come to America
6. How the family business helped them create a home

A formal outline uses indention and numbers to indicate levels of subordination.

Formal sentence outline

Thesis statement: An immigrant must embrace the future and, to some extent reject the past, if he is to create a new home.

   I. Mr. Shin decides the family must leave Korea.
      A. The unstable political climate oppresses the people.
      B. He wants to be in business for himself.
      C. He believes in America as the place of individual liberty.
  II. Mr. Chan plans to leave Thailand.
      A. Political unrest makes him fear for his safety.
      B. He has relatives already in America.
 III. Both immigrants start businesses in America.
      A. Shin starts a computer business.
      B. Chan starts a restaurant.
      C. The businesses buy them freedom to grow and change.
  IV. Both have integrated into their communities.
      A. They live in nice houses.
      B. They are active in church and in civic activities.
      C. Both even are proud to pay taxes.

Formal topic outline

   I. Shin leaves Korea
      A. Political instability
      B. Business
      C. American mythology
  II. Chan leaves Thailand
      A. Political unrest
      B. Relatives in America
 III. Both in business
      A. Shin and computers
      B. Chan and restaurant
      C. Freedom to grow and change
  IV. Identity with community
      A. Houses
      B. Church, civic activities
      C. Americanized, taxes

Writing a first draft

Writers often handicap themselves by assuming that they should write a composition in a certain order—that they should write the first word of the composition first and the last word last. Those writers mistake the order of the words in the completed composition (a product) for the order of the words as they come out in the actual writing (a process). Writing—including all the preliminary steps that we have discussed—usually is anything but straightforward and linear. So the best advice you can give yourself as you begin writing is to begin anywhere you can. Only after you get words on the page can you begin making decisions about revision and altering the content or form of the composition as you wish.

Introductions and conclusions occupy strategic locations in a composition and strongly affect a reader's reaction to the composition. In general they are also harder to write because they differ in function from the rest of the composition. An introduction is the point of entry that arouses a reader's interest and indicates the subject and strategy of the composition. A conclusion satisfactorily completes the essay; it may summarize, restate certain ideas, contain the conclusion of an argument, or point to the other subjects that could be discussed.

The following introductory paragraph grabs the reader's attention and indicates the content, and to some extent the tone (the writer's attitude toward the subject) of the discussion that will follow.

> Broadway, west side, a storefront window, and painted on the plate glass a cup of steaming coffee; morning, Cottonwood Falls, the Emma Chase Café, November: I'm inside and finishing a fine western omelet and in a moment will take on the planks of homemade wheat bread—just as soon as the shadow from the window coffee cup passes across my little notebook.
>
> —William Least Heat Moon, *PrairyErth*

In the body of the essay the author explores the effects of the café on the town and on the women who have worked there. But this introductory paragraph does not indicate the theme of the essay—only the subject and the author's attitude toward that subject. He concludes the essay with a conversation with one of the women who tells what the café taught her and who states one of the themes that has been building in the essay.

> ". . . because of the Emma Chase, I see my femaleness differently; now I think feminism means being connected with other people, not just with other feminists."

This is a dominant theme in the essay—being connected to land and to other people, often by work.

In the following introductory paragraph, the author clearly signals subject and theme. The concluding paragraph restates in different language that theme and points to the future.

Introduction	In middle-class circles these days, one can hardly drop into a conversation or pick up a magazine or skim through a book without encountering sentences that begin: "The trouble with men is . . ." These are not exclusively women's sentences; this is not a sexual class war, with Amazonian feminists launching guerrilla raids upon men. More and more, the accusations also come from men themselves.
Conclusion	The winds of change blew for years before women won the vote, another half-century before the modern feminist movement began. They will have to blow far into the next century, no doubt, before men will have outgrown their troubles.

> —Peter Filene, "Between a Rock and a Soft Place"

The purpose of Filene's essay is to explain and to persuade. By announcing his thesis in the beginning, he establishes his point of view immediately. At the conclusion, he restates the thesis because part of his point is that change will come slowly and incrementally. He means, the reader may assume, to encourage patience and vigilance.

As you read essays in magazines, textbooks, and newspapers, look carefully at the introductory and concluding paragraphs. Examine the strategy involved in writing them and try to discover methods that you are comfortable using.

Avoid using clichés in your introductions. Also avoid unnecessary definitions, such as "Webster defines an emigrant as . . . ." Finally, do not apologize in either your introduction or your conclusion ("Although I am no expert on this subject, I . . ."). Apologies undermine the effectiveness of your paper.

Good titles help establish good first impressions. But they can do much more. They can indicate the tone and content of a composition, and they can pique a reader's interest. The introductory and concluding paragraphs in Filene's essay give one particularly good example. Filene's essay is titled "Between a Rock and a Soft Place." In the introductory paragraph he describes the rock that men are up against and begins to suggest the softer "feminine" side of men that is being encouraged. The title is accurate and a little light-hearted, as if not to take this problem overly seriously. The concluding paragraph revisits these soft and hard images which describe the paradox of being a man in contemporary society. The first and last paragraphs and the title work well together to indicate to the reader the content, the tone, and the shape of the discussion, and the reader is pleased with the symmetry that the writer has achieved.

Revising subsequent drafts

Tone reveals your attitude toward your subject and must be appropriate for your subject, audience, and purpose. In the two following paragraphs, the authors' tones differ sharply although both are exploring the subject of how we can save our environment.

> The world that environs us, that is around us, is also within us. We are made of it; we eat, drink, and breathe it; it is bone of our bone and flesh of our flesh. It is also a Creation, a holy mystery, made for and to some extent by creatures, some but by no means all of whom are humans. This world, this Creation, belongs in a limited sense to us, for we may rightfully require things of it—the things necessary to keep us fully alive as the kind of creature we are; but we also belong to it, and it makes certain rightful claims upon us: that we care properly for it, that we leave it undiminished, not just to our children, but to all the creatures who will live in it after us.
>
> —Wendell Berry, "Conservation Is Good Work"

> Although eco-radicals argue that it is only by personally reconnecting with nature that we can save nature, I would argue that the most ecological course for human society is, in fact, to divorce ourselves, and our economy, from the natural world. Our greatest contributions to the environment will come when we're farthest removed from it—in the laboratory, in the voting booth, and in the marketplace. To advocate this notion, which has been labeled "decoupling," is to acknowledge a profound division that many Greens allege is at the root of the ecological crisis. Yet the technological progress that occurs when we disengage from the natural world has already averted ecological devastation many times. Europe, for example, avoided complete deforestation only because early modern smelters substituted coal for charcoal. The process should continue as composites replace steel and as coal begins to yield to solar power—with nature breathing easier everywhere as a result. One must wonder whether self-proclaimed deep ecologists, affirming their communion with nature through shamanistic rituals, will be in a position to supply the world with solar technologies. I suspect rather that such a contribution

will come, if at all, from high-tech corporations—from firms operating in a social, eco-nomic, and technical milieu largely removed from the intricate webs of the natural world.
—Martin W. Lewis, "The Green Threat to Nature"

Do not think of revision as simply the last stage of composing. Revision plays an impor-tant part in every stage of composition—from the first vague notions about the subject to the last proofreading. During the composing process you will often pause to rethink or to see in a different way some aspect of the paper; each of these acts is a part of revision.

There is, however, some danger of being overly conscious of the need to revise as you write. Some writers become so impressed with the inadequacy of what they have written or are about to write that they freeze up, fall victim to a writer's block, and cannot con-tinue. The best advice to give yourself is to write, to get words on the page that you and your instructor can assess. Until you get the words out of your head and onto a piece of paper, there is very little anyone can do to help you as a writer.

As you revise, ask these questions about the **essay as a whole:**

- Does the whole essay stick to the purpose and the subject?
- Have you kept your audience clearly in mind? Is the tone appropriate and consistent? Do any terms require definition?
- Is the focus consistent? Do the ideas in the essay show clear relationships to the central idea or thesis?
- Is the central idea or thesis sharply conceived? Does your thesis statement (if one is appropriate) clearly suggest the position and approach you are taking?
- Have you chosen an effective method or combination of methods of development?
- Is the essay logically sound both as a whole and in individual paragraphs and sen-tences?
- Will the introduction arouse the reader's interest? Does it indicate what the paper is about?
- Does the essay come to a satisfying close?
- Are all the paragraphs unified? Are there any ideas in any paragraph that do not belong?
- Is each paragraph coherent? Are sentences within each paragraph in a natural and effective order? Are the sentences connected by repetition of key words or ideas, by pronoun reference, by parallel structure, or by transitional expressions?
- Is the progression between paragraphs easy and natural? Are there clear transitions where needed?
- Is each paragraph adequately developed?

Below is a list of questions that you will find useful as you edit. Apply them systemat-ically after you have become satisfied with the overall structure of the essay.

Editor's checklist

Sentences and diction
- Have you used subordination and coordination to relate ideas effectively?
- Are there misplaced parts or dangling modifiers?

- Do you find any faulty parallelism?
- Are there any needless shifts in grammatical structures, in tone or style, or in viewpoint?
- Does each pronoun refer clearly to its antecedent?
- Are ideas given appropriate emphasis within the sentence?
- Are the sentences varied in length? in type?
- Are there any fragments? comma splices or fused sentences?
- Do all the verbs agree with their subjects? pronouns with their antecedents?
- Have you used the appropriate form of the verb?
- Are any words overused? used imprecisely? vague?
- Have all unnecessary words and phrases been eliminated? Have any necessary words been omitted?

Punctuation, spelling, and mechanics

- Are commas and semicolons used where required by the sentence structure? Have superfluous commas been removed?
- Is any end punctuation omitted?
- Are apostrophes and quotation marks placed correctly?
- Are all words spelled correctly?
- Are capitalization, italics, and abbreviations used correctly?
- Is your manuscript in an acceptable form? Have all words been divided correctly at the ends of lines?

Proofreading

- Examine the setup of your page—margins, spacing, headers, and footers.
- Read carefully so that you see what you have actually written or typed and not what you meant to write or type.
- Use your computer to check spelling, but remember that the spell checker is seriously limited. It will not catch misspelled words that are correct for other words. (*Use* typed for *used* or *to* for *too* will go unnoticed by the spell checker.) Nor will it catch words you omit or unintentionally insert.
- Ask for help. Another person often sees your text more clearly than you.
- Remember that if mistakes remain in your draft after proofreading by your software or another person, those mistakes are your responsibility.

Learn from other writers. Watch carefully as other writers write, revise, edit, and proofread. Emulate their successful strategies and practices. After your instructor returns an essay, look at the notations on it and learn from them. Those notations will have been made by someone with much experience as a writer, and they will indicate much about how carefully your instructor has read and assessed your draft. If you do not understand a comment from your instructor, ask for help with it.

Your final draft indicates much about the entire composing process that led to its creation. Your instructor is likely to look at the drafts as a way of assessing your composing process and helping you improve your command of that process. Keep the various drafts of your essays and compare them to identify how you have improved both the essay and the process of its creation.

Limiting a Topic

Name_____ **Score** _____

DIRECTIONS Point out the problems that you might have in writing about the following topics. Evaluate each topic on the basis of its suitability for an essay of 300 to 500 words written for readers like those in your English class.

TOPICS

soap operas
the theory of humor
a theme in Kate Chopin's *The Awakening*
what I have learned from watching television

PROBLEMS

DIRECTIONS Choose one of the general topics listed next and plan a limited essay of 300 to 500 words. Consider your classmates as the audience for your essay. To limit the general topic that you choose, use one of the techniques discussed in this unit or some other technique that you have found useful. Save the work that you do in limiting the topic because your notes will be useful in future exercises.

TOPICS

1. changing gender roles   **6.** Buffy the vampire slayer

2. women writers   **7.** travel literature

3. weddings   **8.** education

4. food   **9.** work

5. Ellis Island   **10.** nature literature

PLAN

Planning the Composition: The Thesis   Exercise 26-2

Name_____ **Score** _____

DIRECTIONS Point out the weaknesses of the following thesis statements. Then use the space below to write your own thesis statement for the limited topic that you chose in Exercise 26-1 or on another topic that your instructor approves.

THESIS STATEMENTS

1. We should participate in Women's History Month activities for three main reasons.

2. We should participate in Black History Month activities for three main reasons.

3. There are three main benefits from having a large Asian community in our city.

4. People who read love poetry are romantic wimps.

THESIS STATEMENT

Planning the Composition: The Outline

Name _____ Score _____

DIRECTIONS Read the following essay carefully and make a topic outline of it.

[1]The story "Friend and Protector" by Peter Taylor invites the reader to decide which character best fits the title. [2]A cursory reading could assign friend and protector status to the family servant Jesse because of his devotion to Uncle Andrew. [3]One also might give the status to Uncle Andrew because of his care of Jesse. [4]Although both are possibilities, Aunt Margaret most accurately portrays the role of friend and protector of Jesse Morton.

[5]Although Margaret and Jesse differ in race and social status, she is his friend. [6]Not only has she known him for many years, but she is well acquainted with his shenanigans. [7]During his many years of service to the family, Jesse's encounters with trouble have become routine. [8]The narrator and nephew says, "By the time I came along Jesse's escapades and my uncle and aunt's reactions to them had become a regular pattern"(139). [9]Aunt Margaret knows Jesse, but she remains loyal to him despite his past.

[10]Jesse is the only one of the black servants to move with the family to Memphis. [11]Because he receives a suspended sentence for his involvement in a murder, everyone assumes that Uncle Andrew has reached an understanding with the judge. [12]Nevertheless, taking him in displays a great deal of allegiance from both Mr. and Mrs. Nelson.

[13]Jesse rewards their loyalty with devoted care to both of them but especially to Uncle Andrew. [14]Despite his devotion to the family Jesse continues to get into trouble with the law and has to be bailed out. [15]On one occasion Jesse becomes involved in the "numbers gang" and has his life threatened. [16]Uncle Andrew has to "rescue him from some room above a pool hall where the rival gang had him cornered" (144).

[17]On the other hand, Aunt Margaret behaves like a mother to Jesse. [18]She wants to know when he is going out for an evening. [19]Perhaps she simply means to control him, but it seems more likely that she desires to shield him from harm. [20]After all, he had come into their employment as little more than a boy and had grown up among them.

[21]The Nelsons differ in their attitude toward Jesse as his troubles continue. [22]Uncle Andrew dismisses him as a "mere nothing" (144). [23]Margaret seems to expect more of Jesse and in some ways to marvel at him. [24]The narrator perceives Aunt Margaret as severe with Jesse. [25]He learns her severity when he too misbehaves and is reprimanded by his aunt. [26]She clearly expects better behavior out of him and Jesse. [27]In a critical scene Aunt Margaret watches Jesse as he works in the garden. [28]She stands immobile and upright, staring intently. [29]"Then she would shake her head sadly—exaggerating the shake so that he wouldn't miss it—and turn her back to the window" (155).

[30]In the climax scene of the story, Jesse has become ill and has lost his mind. [31]He is frightened and nearly violent and tries to hide in Uncle Andrew's office. [32]Much to everyone's surprise, he continually calls Aunt Margaret's name. [33]Margaret comes and with "moist eyes" speaks to Jesse in a voice "utterly sweet and beautiful" (156). [34]As the narrator recognizes, this is an occasion like death, and he is witnessing one old friend saying good-bye to another.

[35]Seeking to get a better look at Jesse, Margaret kneels and peers through the door, and when she sees him, her body goes "perfectly rigid" (157). [36]She has not seen what she hoped to see; but she has seen what she feels compelled to see.

[37]In this last scene her role as friend and protector comes clear. [38]One is led to characterize Margaret in this last scene in terms she uses to describe herself: [39]She is "true blue" (152).

Citations from: Taylor, Peter. *The Collected Stories of Peter Taylor.* New York: Penguin, 1986.

Writing the Whole Composition:
Introductions and Conclusions

Name_____ **Score** _____

DIRECTIONS Using the outline that you completed for Exercise 26-3 as a guide, make notes for a new introduction and conclusion to the essay. Write the new introduction and conclusion in the space below.

INTRODUCTION

CONCLUSION

Writing the Composition

Name_____ **Score** _____

DIRECTIONS Write an outline for an essay of 300 to 500 words on the limited topic you select-
ed earlier or on a topic that your instructor approves. Remember that your outline is only a
guide and that you can change it, add to it, or subtract from it whenever you have reason to
do so. When you have finished the outline, write a rough draft and evaluate your composition
using the checklist below. Make any changes that are needed. Then make a final neat copy of
your work. Be sure to give your essay a title that is suitable to the contents of your essay and
that will make your audience want to read it.

CHECKLIST FOR COMPOSITION

1. Is the title both provocative and appropriate?
2. Does the introduction include the thesis statement or a sentence that suggests the
   thesis? Is the rest of the introduction appropriate, and does it lead smoothly into the
   statement or the suggestion of the thesis?
3. Is the relationship of each paragraph to the thesis clear?
4. Is each controlling idea in each paragraph developed fully enough?
5. Is the essay coherent—that is, does each paragraph flow smoothly into the one that
   follows it? (Compare the first sentence of a paragraph with the last sentence of the
   preceding paragraph.)
6. Does the conclusion make you feel that the composition is complete, that the essay
   has ended where it began, with a restatement of the thesis?
7. Are both the grammar and the punctuation of the composition correct? (Proofread the
   paper at least once for any error that you tend to make frequently.)
8. Are all the words spelled correctly?
9. Is there any wordiness that needs to be eliminated?
10. Does the style seem fluid and clear?

COMPOSITION

Conducting research

Writing papers based on research is different in some important ways from nonresearch papers. The most obvious difference is that you will find, read, and integrate material from other writers and nonprint sources into what you know and wish to write. But notice that "you" remain at the center of this enterprise: your voice, your perspective, your analysis and synthesis of all the material is the critical part of your paper.

If you are to control the research and writing of your paper, you must know the purpose of the paper—just as you do for any paper you compose. You will be doing the research and analyzing and synthesizing it because you have a point to prove, a problem to resolve, or an argument to construct. For example, your instructor may give each student a research problem. In response to that research problem, you may write an expository paper or a persuasive paper. If you write an expository paper it will explain

the nature of the problem,
its causes,
its effects, and
the ways others are responding to it.

Your paper will be persuasive if it

asks readers to recognize that a problem exists,
offers a solution to the problem,
calls on readers to undertake a specific action, or
reconciles conflicting parties.

Of course, many research papers are in some measure both expository and persuasive. If you are conscious of your purpose as a writer, you will be able to effect the correct blend of exposition and persuasion. If you have any doubts about the purpose of your paper (i.e., if you cannot write a succinct and clear statement of your purpose), ask your instructor for help.

A reader approaches your research paper with certain clear expectations. The reader expects you to have

done serious research,
understood what you have discovered,
integrated research data into a paper that is clearly your own,
drawn accurately on the work of others, and
honored academic conventions for citing such work.

There are many systems for taking notes, each with its advantages and limitations. Whatever your system, keep in mind these guidelines:

Create a working bibliography of every source you consult. Make sure you have full bibliographic information for every source.

Clearly identify on every note its source. If you photocopy sources, label them with complete bibliographic information.

As you take notes, label clearly each note as a quotation (perhaps by enclosing it in quotation marks) or as a paraphrase. For quotations and paraphrases, include page numbers from the sources.

Quotations must be exact, including all punctuation, omissions, and errors in the original.

Reading through the sources may spark thoughts in you that will be useful in your paper. Write down those thoughts and clearly label them as your own. Indicate also what source sparked them in you.

The clearest indication that you are in control of your research paper will be the ease with which you integrate the source material into your text. You will wish to integrate the source material smoothly so that it complements your voice, your point of view, and your purpose. Writers who are unacquainted with research paper conventions usually make the mistake of dropping quoted material into their text without introducing it. Writers who are familiar with the process always introduce quoted material.

Ineffective	The recent debate over how to use the nation's oil reserves has been taken up by a senate committee. "The president should release the oil reserves in order to lower gas prices (11)." This quotation from Senator Ed Walsh illustrates the growing outcry that the President use the oil reserves.
Effective	The recent debate over how to use the nation's oil reserves has been taken up by a senate committee. Senator Ed Walsh, who represents Florida, a state dependent on tourism, argues that "the president should release the oil reserves in order to lower gas prices (11)."

The introduction to the quotation provides its context and connects it grammatically and semantically with your text.

Quote only those passages in which the writer has written with surpassing clarity and/or beauty. Or quote passages because you wish to attack their ideas.

You often will paraphrase or summarize a passage for inclusion in your text. When you paraphrase, you say in your own words the meaning of the original passage. Do not make the mistake of using some of the author's words in your paraphrase, and do not modify the original by substituting synonyms. A true paraphrase demonstrates that you understand the meaning of the passage well enough to restate it completely. Remember that a paraphrase must be cited exactly as must a quotation.

A summary is briefer than the original passage (and briefer than a paraphrase) and reflects the writer's main idea without including all the detail necessary to develop the idea. It is highly useful in a research paper because it permits you to include the idea without straying into the finer points of the original discussion. Since you still are borrowing ideas from another source, you will cite and document a summary.

Plagiarism is taking someone else's ideas and/or words and representing them as your own. It is a kind of theft, and it is a serious offense. You must guard against committing plagiarism either intentionally or unintentionally. Carelessness or ignorance are not excuses. If you take material from another source and do not accurately and fully document the borrowing, you are committing plagiarism.

The widespread availability of downloadable papers on the Internet has raised a new temptation for students. To submit a paper that you have not written yourself is an act of intellectual dishonesty and the penalties for it usually are severe. It is easy not to make this mistake—just do your own work. And always ask your instructor for help if you are unsure about matters of citation and documentation.

MLA documentation

The MLA method of citation requires placing citations inside parentheses directly into the text. The parenthetical citations refer to a list of works cited at the end of the paper. Numbered notes, in the style once common at the foot of the page or at the end of the paper, still have a function but only as a way to include supplemental information.

The basic content of a parenthetical citation is the author's last name and the page number of the passage being cited. However, the citation need not include information already included in the text. For example, if you have mentioned the author's name just prior to the passage being cited, the citation needs only the page number. If you think about the method to parenthetical citations, you will be able to decide for yourself what information each citation should contain. The purpose of the citation is to send the reader to the list of works cited with sufficient information to identify your source in the list. Make sure the reader has the information necessary to complete the task.

The list of works cited at the end of a paper includes every source that you used. The following examples illustrate the most common types of bibliographic entries. Consult your handbook for a complete list.

Books

A book with one author

Mack, John E. *A Prince of Our Disorder: The Life of T. E. Lawrence.* Boston: Harvard UP, 1976.

More than one work by the same author

> Kinnell, Galway. *Imperfect Thirst*. Boston: Houghton Mifflin, 1994.
>
> ____. *When One Has Lived a Long Time Alone*. New York: Alfred Knopf, 1990.

A book with two authors

> Zipser, Arthur, and Rose Zipser. *Fire and Grace: The Life of Rose Pastor Stokes*. Athens: University of Georgia Press, 1990.

A book whose author is listed as the editor

> Verburg, Carol. Ed. *The Environmental Predicament*. Boston: Beford Books, 1995.

A republished book

> Corbett, Jim. *The Temple Tiger*. 1954. Bombay: Oxford UP, 1994.

An anonymous book and a book with a translator

> *Beowulf*. Trans. Seamus Heaney. New York: Farrar Straus & Giroux, 2000.

Work (story, poem, play) from an anthology. Use this form also for an article or essay first printed in an anthology

> Wakoski, Diane. "The Ring of Irony." *A New Geography of Poets*. Ed. Edward Field, Gerald Locklin, and Charles Stetler. Fayetteville: Arkansas UP, 1992. 92–95.

For an article or essay that was published elsewhere before being included in an anthology

> Chaika, Elaine. "Grammars and Teaching." *College English*. 39 (1978): 770-83. Rpt. In *Linguistics for Teachers*. Ed. Linda Miller Cleary and Michael D. Linn. New York: McGraw, 1993. 490–504.

Articles

Article in a weekly newspaper or magazine

> Adler, Jerry. "It's Not Easy Being Green." *Newsweek* 28 Dec. 1992: 66.

Article in a daily newspaper. When the city name is not part of the title, it appears in brackets after the title of the newspaper.

> Roland, Tom. "Daydreamin' at the Bluebird." *The Tennessean* [Nashville]. 30 March 2000, sec. F: 1+.

Article in a monthly magazine

> Stewart, Doug. "This Joint Is Jumping." *Smithsonian* March 1999: 60–74.

Article in a scholarly journal

> Seyfarth, Susan. "Arnold Schwarzenegger and Iron John: Predator to Protector." *Studies in Popular Culture* XV:1 (1992): 75–81.

An editorial

> Charen, Mona. "Sin eliminated from vocabulary." Editorial. *Daily News Journal* [Murfreesboro, TN] 31 March 2000, A4.

Citing electronic publications

A document within a scholarly project or database

"This Day in Automotive History: April 1." The History Channel Online. 1 April 2000 <http://www.historychannel.com>.

"Adams, Ansel." *Britannica Online*. 30 April 1999. <http://www.britannica.com/bcom/eb/article/8/0,5716,3698+1,00.html>.

A personal or professional site

Lavery, David. "The Owen Barfield World Wide Web Site." 20 October 1999 <http://www.mtsu.edu/~dlavery/Barfield/>.

An article in an online periodical

Bohlen, Celestine. "Yeltsin Resigns, Naming Putin as Acting President to Run in March Election." *New York Times on the Web* 1 January 2000. 30 March 2000 <http://www.nytimes.com/library/world/europe/010100russia-politics.html>.

A publication on a CD-ROM

"Zebra." *The Oxford English Dictionary*. 2nd ed. CD-ROM. Oxford: Oxford UP, 1992.

An email

White, Gwen. "Southern Lit." Email to Larry Mapp. October 27, 2002.

MLA Citations

Name_____ Score _____

DIRECTIONS The following descriptions include sufficient information for creating complete citations, as if for a working bibliography or works cited list. Use the information to create the citation for each description.

EXAMPLE

The novel <u>The Devil's Dream</u> by Lee Smith published in 1992 by Putnam in New York.

Smith, Lee. <u>The Devil's Dream.</u> New York: Putnam, 1992.

1. An article entitled "Politics and the Self in Robert Penn Warren's Poetry" written by Fred R. Thiemann. Appearing in *South Atlantic Review,* Volume 61, Number 4, Fall 1996, on pages 83–96.

2. A collection of essays edited by David Lavery and entitled *This Thing of Ours,* published by Columbia University Press in New York, 2002.

3. A poem published in the annual journal *Poems & Plays,* issue number 10, Spring/Summer 2003, entitled "Only If It's About Me," by Claudia Barnett, on pages 59–60.

4. A presentation entitled "Film Noir," accessed June 4, 2002 on the third disc of a four-disc DVD *American Cinema,* produced by Image Entertainment of 1995.

5. An email from Angela Hague to Claudia Barnett, subject "Iris Murdoch's Fondness for Limpets," sent and received on December 1, 2002.

6. An article in *USA Today,* February 5, 2002, entitled "Summer in Vermont," appearing in section D, page 3, and written by Victoria Clausi.

7. An article in *The New York Times on the Web* entitled "Thousands Vote Online in Arizona," written by Rebecca Fairley Raney, dated March 8, 2000 and accessed on January 23, 2003, at this URL: http://www.nytimes.com/library/tech/00/03/cyber/articles/09vote.html.

8. An article in the monthly *Gourmet,* entitled "Tsar Power," written by Jan Morris and appearing in the February 2003 issue on pages 98–105.

9. An anonymously written novel entitled *Primary Colors,* published in New York by Warner Books in 1996.

10. A Web site entitled *Shamash: The Jewish Network* accessed on January 22, 2003, at this URL: http://shamash.org/.

Paraphrasing and Summarizing

Name_____ Score _____

DIRECTIONS Practice by summarizing and paraphrasing each of the following passages. Be prepared to discuss the differences between summaries and paraphrases and to defend your efforts at each.

EXAMPLE

We cannot get along without symbols, it would be unthinkable. But they are full of strange power and can destroy us quickly when used improperly—as the Germans' experience with them demonstrated. They need to be handled as carefully as nuclear energy and the rules for doing so should be learned by all. Symbols should be kept in their place; they should not be mixed with facts and then treated as though they were facts; nor should facts be mixed with symbols and treated as though they are symbols. (244)

From
Smith, Lillian. *Killers of the Dream*. New York: Norton, 1994.

Paraphrase

Lillian Smith wisely cautions against confusing symbols with facts. Since neither possesses the characteristics of the other, confusing them can lead to a detachment from reality, a corruption of right and wrong, and can lead to some horrible consequences, as the holocaust of World War II reminds us (244).

Summary

We should recall Lillian Smith's reminder that symbols are not facts and should not be treated as if they were facts (244), when we hear the annual cries from a few politicians for a constitutional amendment to ban burning of the flag.

1. The most important concept Rockefeller bequeathed to philanthropy was that of wholesale giving, as opposed to small, scattershot contributions. (238)

From
Chernow, Ron. *Titan: The Life of John Rockefeller, Sr.* New York: Vintage, 1998.

Paraphrase

Summary

2. O'Neill has not left us a single example of a prudent yet spirited man, the sort of figure who in traditional comedies arranges for the emergence of an improved community. His politicians (if that is the word for such ineffectual dreamers as are depicted in *The Iceman Cometh*) merely recast Edmund's dream of cosmic absorption in the form of apocalyptic social renovation—a new heaven and earth peopled with happy socialist workers. (82)

From
Alvis, John. "On the American Line: O'Neill's *Mourning Becomes Electra* and the Principles of the Founding." 22:1 (January 1986): 69–85.

Paraphrase

Summary

3. Star Wars taken as a whole story and viewed in chronological order, is not really the story of Luke at all but the story of Luke's father, Anakin Skywalker, and how he, a Jedi Knight, was corrupted by the dark side of the force and became Darth Vader. When I asked Lucas what Star Wars was ultimately about, he said, "Redemption." He added, 'The scripts to the films that I'm finishing now are a lot darker than the second three, because they are about a fall from grace. The first movie is pretty innocent, but it goes downhill from there, because it's more of a tragic story—that's built into it." (158–59)

From
Seabrook, John. *Nobrow*. New York: Knopf, 2000.

Paraphrase

Summary